ERICH PRZYWARA AND POSTMODERN NATURAL LAW

ERICH PRZYWARA

AND POSTMODERN

NATURAL LAW

A History of the Metaphysics of Morals

GRAHAM JAMES McALEER

University of Notre Dame Press

Notre Dame, Indiana

University of Notre Dame Press
Notre Dame, Indiana 46556
undpress.nd.edu
Copyright © 2019 by the University of Notre Dame

Published in the United States of America

Library of Congress Control Number: 2019948584

ISBN 978-0-268-10593-8 (hardback)
ISBN 978-0-268-10594-5 (paperback)
ISBN 978-0-268-10596-9 (WebPDF)
ISBN 978-0-268-10595-2 (Epub)

∞ This is printed on acid-free paper.

To my teacher at London,

Brian O'Shaughnessy (1925–2010)

CONTENTS

PREFACE

Has modernity failed? The front page of Liverpool Football Club's website declares its commitment to antislavery. It lays out its method for ensuring that none of its clothing and merchandising stems from the work of slaves. And just to remind you, the year is 2018. It is usual to date modernity from Descartes, so we are nearing four hundred years of modernity. In its self-conception, modernity was the offer of clear and evident principles that would free peoples and make them eager to communicate globally to share the best ideas and the earth's wealth. Obviously, conscience has yet to receive those clear directives. Indeed, we seem perplexed by a host of issues. There are more besides, but here are the moral problems I discuss in this book: robots, fashion, Islam and sumptuary laws, Nazism (fascism and race), rule of law and the managerial state, embryos, family, migration, body modification, nature, vanity and extremes of wealth, establishment, and subversion.

My starting point is the greatest work of Thomism in the twentieth century. No fanfare accompanied the first English translation of *Analogia Entis (AE)*, an astonishing work of philosophy and theology.[1] Published in 1932, and in expanded form in 1962, this massive six-hundred-page book was written by the German Polish Jesuit Erich Przywara (1889–1972). *AE* has been quietly shaping Catholic thought for years. Because it is written in a forbidding version of German, few Anglophone intellectuals had access to the book until 2014. Growing up in German intellectual circles, the great intellectual popes Saint John Paul and Benedict XVI were influenced by Przywara. Both mention the book, but only now can most of us appreciate just how deep was its influence.

What follows is a commentary on *AE* but not an exegesis. Copying the style of Francisco de Vitoria's expansive commentaries on Aquinas,

I want to apply Przywara's conceptual framework to the development of the West's thoughtscape and its contemporary problems. I offer an analysis of medieval and modern Western thought in the spirit of the school of Saint Thomas to show that natural law can remedy our failing humanism.

I *update* Przywara by applying his highly suggestive decapitation argument—his observation that there is a strange recurring disembodiment in Western thought—to some of today's moral controversies. My commentary *adds* to the examples of decapitation given by Przywara and confirms his argument about patterns of thought in the West: a sign that *AE* is a great theoretical work is that it helps readers do better exegesis of other thinkers. I hope also to *simplify AE. AE* is not for a general readership. Most Catholic philosophers and theologians I speak with think the book demands too much investment of time and attention. My commentary *extends AE* by making explicit its method of moral inquiry, which is rather muted in the text itself: this might be best characterized as a value-phenomenology of civilizations atop a metaphysics of morals. I call it a liturgy of morals and propose a new account of natural law.

Throughout I address contemporary moral problems and apply Przywara to identify the conceptual patterns active within them: in each case, value confusion follows on metaphysical confusion. With Przywara, I argue that ethical reflection must include a metaphysics of morals. Focusing on patterns of thinking requires in-depth treatment of thinkers other than Przywara—among others, Peter John Olivi, Thomas Reid, Arthur Schopenhauer, and Giorgio Agamben—but the point is always to show the reach of Przywara's model. It is a sign of a great thinker that you can take his ideas on the road, so to say, and resolve topics he did not address by applying his logic. A good example of this phenomenon is Michel Foucault's biopolitics, and I believe intellectuals can turn to Przywara's decapitation insight with equal confidence.

As I explain in more detail in the introduction, *AE* argues that metaphysicians repeatedly tend toward disembodiment and thus proffer false humanisms. This results from a failure to think analogically. Metaphysical positions tend to flip rapidly between univocity and equivocity, a commitment to unity or plurality, or a monism of mind or monism of body. In either case, head is severed from body, and accounts of nature and person offer too much mentalism and too little embodiment, or vice versa. In fact, what Przywara is keen to show, and does so successfully, I believe, is that the same metaphysical theory whips back and forth between each of these two poles, exhibiting instability, with disastrous moral and political consequences.

Though hard to believe given the depth of historical evidence that shows the tight knotting between medieval and modern thought, a survey of most college professors would deliver one batch who think Middle Ages bad, modernity good, and another (much smaller) batch who think modernity bad, Middle Ages good. Much of this has to do with contemporary politics and the culture wars between progressives and the Catholic Church. Consider that a typical introductory university course on philosophy is likely to move along a line: Greek thought (pure philosophy), medieval thought (religious intrusion into philosophy), Enlightenment thought (secularization and purifying philosophy of religion), postmodernity (nihilism). And the victor is? Liberalism: pure philosophy delivering universal rights!

By contrast, Przywara argues that Christianity is the truth of metaphysics (*AE,* 307), that in the Incarnation and the suffering of Christ what exists is revealed. *AE* is an argument that not only is Christianity true but the Incarnation commits one to Catholicism. Christian theology is fraught and *AE* tries to show how the history of theology falls into the same familiar patterns one finds in secular thinking. Its argument is not Christian theology good, secularism bad. Plato and Aristotle are heroes in *AE,* though a high-water mark is reached with Aquinas (*AE,* 306). Thereafter, in the Middle Ages itself, and in modernity, there is a falling away from Thomas's metaphysical humanism. However, Przywara does not argue that modern thinkers are benighted: only that they oftentimes emphasize parts of metaphysics to the detriment of others, while a true humanism requires the parts be held in tension. Przywara offers dozens of interpretations of modern thinkers, as well as modern cultural movements, in an effort to pick out what is positive. His thinking is not dialectical but reconciling, and he picks out elements of theorists that can reveal the "in-and-beyond" structure of creatureliness. This reconciling approach predates Przywara, with leading lights of the school of St. Thomas—thinkers of the stature of Jean Capreolus and de

Vitoria—making use of arguments from other thinkers: I do the same throughout, relying on people like Thomas Reid and Edmund Burke to make my arguments.

As do many of the most significant twentieth-century Catholic thinkers, Przywara singles out phenomenology as a crucial and positive development in modern thought. He treats Husserl and Heidegger warily but admires Scheler. He quietly favors Scheler's moral realism, his arguments that reality is populated with hierarchically arranged values. Just as de Vitoria makes a wide-ranging application and development of Thomas, so too do I want to deploy Przywara in light of value phenomenology. Along with Karol Wojtyla, I think there is a way to explain natural law with reference to what we might call a phenomenology of value tones. I develop this line of natural law reflection in *Ecstatic Morality and Sexual Politics* (2005), *To Kill Another* (2010), *Tolkien and* Lord of the Rings*: A Philosophy of War* (2014), and *Veneration and Refinement* (2016). In those works, I argue that natural law is Christoform. I will not rehearse arguments I make in those books here but Proverbs 8:30–31 speaks of the Word at creation playing before the Father and delighting him. The play character of God's sovereignty echoes in establishment and the rules of games. Rule of law, swathed in pageantry, expresses the origin of natural inclination in the decorous play that is Christ (*AE*, 279). This is the "in-and-beyond" character of creatureliness that Przywara believes the church captures in its doctrine of the *analogia entis*. This is what *Postmodern Natural Law* aims to show.

The book has two parts. The first five chapters, covering the Middle Ages through postmodernism, are historical studies in the metaphysics of morals. In the final three chapters, I develop a liturgy of morals.

After introducing Przywara's metaphysical framework, the first chapter treats Robert Kilwardby's account of the Incarnation. It is an example of decapitation within Catholic medieval theology. For metaphysical reasons, Kilwardby views the divinity of Christ as surfing above the tribulations of Christ's human nature. He resists a thorough embodiment of the Word, and he does so, I argue, for reasons of political theology: his angelism is a dissent from the theological anthropology of the Gregorian Reform. His metaphysics of the Incarnation expresses skepticism about Pope Gregory VII's hope in the salutary character of human institutions.

Robert's skepticism is common among theologians to this day and makes problematic any humanism. Chapter 2 identifies another theme of decapitation in medieval theology: the effort to explain the disembodied sensations of the damned. Giles of Rome and Peter John Olivi developed an angelism that had far-reaching consequences in Western thinking. In chapter 3, I argue that this debate was responsible for the growth of idealism and a tendency toward angelism in Enlightenment philosophy. I discuss the reaction to this angelism in the thinking of Reid and Schopenhauer. This third chapter is pivotal, for I argue that Reid's account of natural language—which ties body and value intuition together—is an important avenue of thought for natural law reasoning and diverges dramatically from the vitalist decapitation one finds in Schopenhauer and, later, in Nazi anthropology.

In my opinion, Aurel Kolnai's *War against the West* definitively shows that a German tradition of biocentrism, stretching back at least to Schopenhauer, gave National Socialism a ready platform for its race anthropology. I examine this example of decapitation in chapter 4. Postmodernism is a reaction to the failings of modernity, and in chapter 5, I examine two contemporary thinkers I admire very much, Giorgio Agamben and D. G. Leahy. These postmodernists explicitly return to the problem of angels but again fall foul of Przywara's logic: this explains how their arguments about angels (mind) end up as arguments about clothes (body). Their discussion about the ontology of clothes leads into chapter 6, where I explore Merleau-Ponty's late phenomenology in light of his persistent use of the images of clothing to explain his concept of the flesh. One aim is to show that his criticism of Scheler's value phenomenology fails, but a second and more important goal is to show how Merleau-Ponty reiterates Reid's insight about the gestural body and intuition of value tones. This is the first chapter of the second part of the book, where I offer a fresh statement of my elaboration of natural law.[2]

In chapters 7 and 8, I offer a formal account of natural law in light of value ethics. As I mention above, in the manner of Karol Wojtyla, I have elsewhere linked natural law with a theory of value tones. While it is hardly expressed explicitly, I think Przywara's value phenomenology of civilizations is similar. I argue that posture, gesture, dress-ups, ritual, and play— a liturgy of morals—are basic to ethics. Ethical formalism has no traction in the absence of liturgies, which are themselves responsive to nonformal value tones. I conclude that humanism cannot be sustained without Christoform natural law. I thus twin natural law and political theology: a Christian metaphysics of morals in support of humanistic civilization.

I hope this book will turn people into readers of Przywara: the publication in English of his text is set to accelerate its quiet but profound shaping of Catholic thought. About reading Przywara, a word of warning. Hegel and Lacan are notoriously difficult authors, and I have not read a more difficult book than *AE*. The translation is a truly heroic collaboration of two friends, John Betz, a theologian at the University of Notre Dame, and David Bentley Hart, a writer well known to those who read the Christian intellectual magazine *First Things*. Theirs is a remarkable accomplishment.

Why bother trying to read such a difficult book? It will frustrate everyone who picks it up, and most will promptly put it down. However, for those with patience and a willingness to read the text many times, astonishing things await. Quite beyond the span of the history of philosophy and theology, unique thoughts on law, marriage, art, politics, history, and civilization, await the dedicated reader. A more positive way of expressing the book's difficulty is to say that no single work by a Catholic in the twentieth century rivals the book in scope or insight.

A huge thanks must go to John Betz, my colleague when he was at Loyola, whose long introduction to *AE* is an excellent road map for coming to grips with the text, as well as the historical background to Przywara's life and interactions with other intellectuals of the twentieth century. I also want to thank Paul Seaton, Alex Rosenthal, Meghan Page, Fr. John Peck, S.J., Fr. Brendan Fitzgerald, Lauren Weiner, and especially Chris Wojtulewicz. Special thanks both to Jim Buckley of Loyola's Department of Theology, for daring to teach with me the *Analogia Entis* to undergraduates, and to those undergraduates who tolerated our fascination with this difficult book. Special thanks also to Marion Wielgosz, who has always taken such care to tidy my manuscripts.

It remains to thank my wife, Jennifer, and my children, Julia, Charlotte, and Beatrice.

ABBREVIATIONS

In citing works in the notes, short titles have generally been used. Works frequently cited have been identified in the text by the following abbreviations:

AE   Erich Przywara. *Analogia Entis: Metaphysics; Original Structure and Universal Rhythm.* Translated by John R. Betz and David Bentley Hart. Grand Rapids: Eerdmans, 2014.

Beyond   D. G. Leahy. *Beyond Sovereignty: A New Global Ethics and Morality.* Aurora, CO: Davies Group, 2010.

Foundation D. G. Leahy. *Foundation: Matter the Body Itself.* Albany: SUNY Press, 1996.

FR   Arthur Schopenhauer. *On the Fourfold Root of the Principle of Sufficient Reason.* Translated by D. E. Cartwright, E. E. Erdmann, and C. Janaway. Cambridge: Cambridge University Press, 2012.

IE   Thomas Reid. *Inquiry and Essays.* Indianapolis: Hackett, 1983.

KG   Giorgio Agamben. *The Kingdom and the Glory.* Stanford, CA: Stanford University Press, 2011.

PVNS   Aurel Kolnai. *Politics, Values, and National Socialism.* London: Transaction, 2013.

QN   Peter John Olivi. *Quaestiones de novissimis ex summa super IV sententiarum.* Edited by P. Maranesi. Rome: Editiones Collegii S. Bonaventurae, 2004.

II *Sent.*   Robert Kilwardby. *Quaestiones in lib. II Sententiarum.* Edited by G. Leibold. Munich: Bayerische Akademie der Wissenschaften, 1992.

III *Sent.*   Robert Kilwardby. *Quaestiones in lib. III Sententiarum.* Edited by E. Gossmann. Munich: Bayerische Akademie der Wissenschaften, 1982.

ST   Thomas Aquinas. *Summa theologica.*

VI   Maurice Merleau-Ponty. *The Visible and the Invisible.* Evanston, IL: Northwestern University Press, 1968.

VS   John Paul II. *Veritatis Splendor.* Encyclical. 1993. http://w2 .vatican.va/content/john-paul-ii/en/encyclicals/documents /hf_jp-ii_enc_06081993_veritatis-splendor.html.

WAW   Aurel Kolnai. *The War against the West.* London: Victor Gollancz, 1938.

WWR   Arthur Schopenhauer. *The World as Will and Representation.* 2 vols. Translated by E. F. J. Payne. New York: Dover, 1969.

INTRODUCTION

Many will recall the media storm provoked by Pope Benedict's Regensburg address, "Faith, Reason and the University."[1] Delivered in Germany in 2006, it was widely perceived as supporting George W. Bush and the second Iraq war. Incendiary was Benedict's quote from a Byzantine emperor that the Koran brought nothing new save "there you will find things only evil and inhuman, such as his command to spread by the sword the faith he preached." What is now obvious is that the scholarly Benedict wrote his Regensburg address as a commentary on *Analogia Entis* (*AE*).

In no way does this fresh insight on "Faith, Reason and the University" preclude it from also having been a political document. *AE* ranges across the classic domains of philosophy (epistemology, metaphysics, logic, language, and value theory) and Christian theology (creation, salvation history, scripture, the church, and liturgy). Throughout the book, however, a fascinating reflection on moral, legal, and political theory unfolds.

"Faith, Reason and the University" sets out to clarify the logic of religious, as well as secular, terrorism. Benedict deploys Przywara's central argument: a proper accounting of the relationship between God and nature defers to the analogy of being (*analogia entis*). Islam errs in arguing that God's law is sovereign, having no continuity with the human understanding of natural, customary, or civil law. These latter kinds of law are not analogous to God's law but equivocal, or, in other words, not really law at all. In Islam, all law is revelation. Inverting this entirely is the modern, Enlightenment tradition of law that reason is adequate to the discernment of the common good, and no supplement to civil law is necessary, whether from nature, custom, or God. According to this view, human law is not analogous to God's law but univocal, straightforwardly replacing the divine.

Where the logic of law is equivocal or univocal, terror ensues. No rational clarification of divine law is possible on the first view, for all human judgment of the divine is presumption. Terror answers those who dare to search out God's utterly transcendent ways. The rationalist is equally intolerant. Law is rational: any failure to comply must be due to perversity and a malign interest in subversion of the patently obvious. History is replete with shocking examples of rationalists terrorizing kind and thoughtful people, who did not think simple rationality adequate to human experience.

Requisite is an understanding that the varieties of law, whether stemming from divine or human will, natural order, or settled community practice, are analogical. All are valid law, necessitating careful adjudication of their respective scope and where best to place emphasis, so that the common good might prevail. Since 1215 and the Fourth Lateran Council, Catholic adjudication of these varied claims has been rooted in the analogy of being. Przywara wrote, "The language proper to the mind of the church is one of an aristocratic and sober distance from the 'enthusiasms' of Charismatics, Pneumatics . . . the same distance expressed by the Council of Trent's rejection of the Reformation, by the church's edicts against Jansenism, by the Vatican Council's rejection of Romanticism, and by the church's edicts against modernism" (*AE,* 374–75). Benedict's address prefers this "ecclesial discretion" (*AE,* 374) to the destructive contemporary enthusiasms plaguing East and West. This discretion is rooted in a metaphysics and liturgy of morals.

Imagine a suspension bridge with only one pillar. The pillar is God and the bridge is all of creation in structured motion. Yonder is nothing, or what Przywara calls the "demonism of negative boundlessness" (*AE,* 314). God's decision to create is the "binding origin" of creation, a realm of service (*AE,* 236). God's decision creates the span of the bridge, all of which is a *potentia obedientialis* to God's actuality. This is the relationship between *is* and *not*. Metaphysically, it captures the greatest degree of dissimilarity between God's autonomous agency and the prostration of everything else. However, God's utter gratuity founds another metaphysical relationship, in which a degree of similarity exists between creator and creature. The decision of God to span the is/not in the gift of actuality to the not gives a degree of actuality to the not and thus a similarity between creature and Creator is born. And therewith, an astonishing similarity between creature and Creator comes into sight: spanning potentiality and actuality, the creature possesses an agency over itself, a structure able, to a degree, to choreograph motion of self and other. In the technical language of scholasticism, the creature is a secondary cause; it shares an attribute with God, for both are active causes shaping potency (*analogia attributionis*). This similarity thins as the creature has standing only as a cause because its nature is *derived* from an *underived* gifting source (*analogia proportionis*). It fades finally in what Przywara calls "play" (*AE*, 307): the mystery of God's decision to gift his standing in any degree whatever and to then reaffirm the spanning in the mystery of the Incarnation (*analogia entis*).

To my knowledge, Przywara is unique in claiming that Aquinas's metaphysics was crafted as a defense of the Fourth Lateran Council of 1215, which gave to the church the formula "One cannot note any similarity between creator and creature, however great, without being compelled to observe an ever greater dissimilarity between them" (*AE*, 73). Przywara believes this formula is not only the heart of Catholic consciousness but is the truth of metaphysics as such. It is a yardstick of metaphysical theories, and *AE* is a tour de force—Przywara sweeping the history of metaphysics to show how, again and again, metaphysicians slip away from analogy to defend either univocity or equivocity. Further, as such positions are false, they are also unstable: the univocal position flips into the equivocal and vice versa within one and the same metaphysical theory.

Przywara examines this whiplash phenomenon in a variety of thinkers, but consider two he does not speak about. Bishop George Berkeley literally has a metaphysics that is only mind and no body, but his thought shuttles between cohesion and dispersion: minds that are cohesive substances (univocity) and objects of mind that are constellations of episodic perceptions cohering as objects only through language (equivocity). For

Arthur Schopenhauer, the core of reality is a monistic will (univocity) that breaks into shards of mutually antagonistic objects for mind (equivocity), only for mind to self-oblate and reduce the multiplicity of world back to oneness of will (univocity). I discuss each of these modern thinkers more (chapter 3) after exploring the same phenomenon in the work of medieval theologians.

Only analogy can hold the emphases of univocal and equivocal thinking in the correct tension, so that they sway together rather than fly apart (*AE*, 426–27). Let me give a summary of the metaphysical commitments of a univocal and an equivocal metaphysics. This is Przywara's diagnostic tool, which he uses to assess the failure of modernity's humanism, the power of which we will observe in a recent discussion of robotics.

Without analogy, it is easy for thought to stress either structure or motion. From the beginning of the history of metaphysics, thinkers have been struck by things changing but in an orderly fashion. Among the pre-Socratics, Parmenides stressed order and Heraclitus motion. The stresses are there in reality, but each thinker exaggerated and set up a dialectical whiplash at the start of the West's reflection on reality.

In light of Parmenides, metaphysics stresses mind, ideal, a priori, one, unity, stability, and essence. Theologically, this tendency is theopanism, the idea "God is all." It is an emphasis on Sophia. Thinkers tending toward Parmenides include Plato, Augustine, Dionysius, Descartes, Kant, and Husserl. In light of Heraclitus, we have a counterimage: body, material, a posteriori, many, difference, movement, and existence. Theologically, the counterimage produces pantheism—the idea "all is God." The emphasis is on philo. Thinkers tending toward Heraclitus include Aristotle, Thomas, Hume, Nietzsche, Heidegger, and Foucault.

Parmenides's "all in one" is univocity and stresses the unity of things in a yonder beyond change. Theologically, it offers only "an emptied theology" (*AE*, 164), a formal, sterile divinity (imagine the angels singing atonal compositions). Crucially, for Przywara, this divine beyond is part of philosophy and metaphysics, not an import from theology. Put differently, the modern liberal habit of thinking of philosophy and theology as sui generis different falsifies the first impulse of philosophical reflection (*AE*, 161). Heraclitus's "all is change" is equivocity and puts a stress on the strangeness of one thing from another: pluriformity, chaotic desire (in music, chromaticism). Theologically, this is apostasy and sectarianism and delight in myth (*AE*, 166). The tedious liberal who thinks religion is an intrusion on an independent-minded pristine philosophy falsifies thought's original seeking out of strangeness, the grotesque, and the uncanny (*AE*, 505, 523).

In Przywara's own lifetime, he witnessed the absolutizing of these two metaphysical stresses. In Russia, he observed the messianic welcome of Leninism—politics as pure thought, salvation offered through rational planning, the ultimate tensions of life resolved through panopticon government. Marxist totalitarianism drove entire peoples into an abyss of suffering. In Germany, he saw the messianic welcome of Hitlerism—politics of pure urge, salvation through immersion in strife, the ultimate tensions of life resolved through lurid fantasies fostered by government. National Socialist totalitarianism also drove entire peoples into an abyss of suffering.

How did metaphysics create a platform for these horrors? The killings followed on metaphysical decapitation: univocity head equivocity body (*AE*, 257). It is no surprise that Marxism and National Socialism failed as humanism, as neither concerned itself with a unified person, head, and body. Kolnai warned that progressive democracy fairs little better, and in 1950, he predicted that Western liberal democracies would collapse into medicalized dictatorships. Consider the exploitation of early human life: the embryo. On the one hand, we are told embryos have no rights because they have no heads (univocity). They are not sentient, nor do they have personal agency needing respect. On the other hand, they are the most cherished of all things. Their stem cells are pluriform and can grow to make any body part. They are, in principle, the total human (equivocity). As the embryo has no personal form or structure (univocity), its parts can be stripped out (equivocity) and made to serve and perpetually regenerate true human lives (gods!).

When a woman, having sought out in vitro fertilization, wishes to memorialize the embryos she did not carry to term, an Australian jeweler will entomb the embryo in a reliquary to grace ankle, wrist, or neck. Moral confusion abounds. For the secular, this is a trade in the macabre, akin to Victorians taking photographs beside their dead loved ones.[2] There is an obvious disanalogy that the jeweler herself is close to seeing, when she argues that her art houses the sacred. On this account, her business would be close to simony: selling spiritual gifts.[3] Later, I discuss the moral stand-ing of human skin clothes (see chapter 6), but this is a step beyond: this jewelry houses the sacred because it involves the taking of human life. The women involved are not indifferent to these early humans but are not averse to killing them either. How is this metaphysically possible? This commerce in early human life follows on metaphysical decapitation.

Both attitudes are present in in vitro fertilization and are at the root of this jewelry trade. The embryo is venerated in a reliquary because of its structure: its sibling, after all, is a beautiful cherished baby, and the entombed could just as easily have been chosen for birth instead of its sibling (univocity). But because it is potent biological material, it can be used instrumentally—it is actually a human being conceived as property (a slave), ready to be mastered and retooled (equivocity).

The liberal metaphysics of the embryo is an incoherent mess, except that it is what Przywara predicted. Without the *analogia entis*, which spans and holds in tension both univocity and equivocity, each with their cor-rect insight into structure and change, metaphysics whips back and forth between the two—a univocal system flipping over into equivocity and vice versa. The whole is unsettled, valuing and disvaluing an object at the same time, and unable to sustain a true humanism or civilizational act.

Let us see how all this coalesces in the contemporary discussion of robots. Transhumanism is both very new and very, very old. Whether it is the promise of a chip that when worn will immediately report the start of cancer cells in your body or an artificial intelligence "doctor" diag-nosing you from data your handheld device collects when you are jolted with a pang of sciatica, transhumanism recalls the very origin of clothes, the cowrie shells worn about the waist to ward off the "evil eye."

The problem for transhumanism, however, is that the evil eye is built into its metaphysics. By this I do not mean the plausible thesis that tech-nology has ends of its own quite distinct from human ones,[4] or that ro-bots are bound to come and get us (see the super film *Ex Machina*), but rather that transhumanism has absorbed a warped metaphysics that kneecaps its soteriological promise. It will not save us from the evil eye because transhumanism takes its bearings from our decapitation.

Transhumanist writer Yuval Harari interestingly argues that transhu-manism is birthing two new religions, techno-humanism and dataism.[5]

Techno-humanism aims to make us superhuman by transforming us into cyborgs, reframing our bodies with digital biomechanics. In this religion, humans are squarely the gods, our desires and interests furthered by physical enhancement.

The second religion is dataism, which, unlike techno-humanism, unmasks us and puts us firmly in our place. This religion teaches that humans are currently just the planet's most sophisticated data-processing units but will soon be made redundant by far better ones. This point is ceded once people allow algorithms to shape their dating lives, suspend their capacity to read maps, or become their stylists.[6] We look up to a new god in dataism; we celebrate ourselves as gods in techno-humanism.

With Plato, metaphysical systems put a stress on the mind, or with Aristotle, on the body. As we saw, Przywara actually pushed these options further back, linking Plato to Parmenides (all is one) and Aristotle to Heraclitus (change is all). It certainly is uncanny the way that Harari sees robotics offering one or the other of these options. Dataism thinks of us as a head only and is heir to Plato, while techno-humanism seeks to reframe our bodies and is heir to Aristotle. But what exactly is bad about decapitation? What is the loss in being a headless body or a head without a body?

At one time, an obvious and adequate answer needing no defense would have been the loss is our humanity. What this answer assumes is that being whole—an ordered unity of head and body—is aspirational. Our moral tradition assumes it: reason and the passions need alignment. Transhumanism puts in question whether this is precisely right, questioning whether there is any great loss without the whole. As tech writers point out, we are already, and seemingly happily, siding with one or the other of these new faiths, rapidly embracing our partibility as whim takes us.

Is decapitation a problem to be solved? Decapitation certainly sounds bad, but philosophers have been misled by appearances before. Przywara argued that the reasons to be concerned are at once metaphysical, epistemological, political, and civilizational. We turn again to totalitarianism.

The twentieth century witnessed frenzied political movements that gleefully embraced the Heraclitean world of bodily energy in constant movement, with awful consequences for politics and civilization (Fascism). Przywara—a firsthand witness—was equally concerned with the challenge such a metaphysics posed to the structures of thought itself.

The problem with the claim that we are radically embodied and closed in a world of perpetual and unrestrained change is that truth and falsity blend into one another. This means that the fulcrum of thought, the principle of noncontradiction—one cannot affirm of the same thing in the same respect that it is true and not true—is suspended (*AE*, 195–96). The problem with being a headless body is that the norms of rationality and argument are overthrown, exposing all to the highest quanta of the will to power. The metaphysics of techno-humanism creates not gods but victims, slaves, or nations that need to draw on all their civilizational reserves to uproot such tyranny.

The twentieth century also witnessed deluded political movements that somberly embraced the Parmenidian world of ideas and ruthlessly broke traditional communities, and entire peoples even, on the wheel of joyless logical systems (Communism). That these movements purported to love the people, which was utter cynicism, Przywara argued, was to be expected: if all is one, then truth and falsity, being and nonbeing, are ultimately, and indifferently, the same. The irony could not be greater, for here too, the principle of noncontradiction is suspended. Logical system is evacuated of rationality or practical wisdom and with entirely predictable results: a turn to brutish assertion of power.

The metaphysics of Dataism offers only a cruel god committed to ridding the world of the ludic, festive, and barnaclelike irregularities and compromises that have shaped human communities down through the ages. A metaphysics of the head always boils down to political arrangements that, as Adam Smith warned, seek to move individuals as though they are pieces on a chessboard.

Przywara argued that Christian theology, though it often gets the stress wrong, is wedded to the idea that humans are rational creatures owing their existence to a beneficent designer mightier than they. This valorizes the mind, but the core of Christianity, the Incarnation, thoroughly affirms the dignity of the body. In confirming that mind and body belong together, the Incarnation clarifies that divine healing perfects human nature, neither removing nor ignoring it. Edmund Burke makes the Incarnation into the political insight that establishment funnels political passions (body) into the collected intelligence of a community's historical political leadership (mind).

Intriguingly, transhumanism does not dispute that the human being is a "religious animal" (Burke). It promises a purifying deluge, but its version of the biblical flood will not deliver a pristine new creation. Neither cyborg armor nor a geometric future can deliver on their salvific promise, for each rests on human partibility. Przywara ably shows that tyranny will fill the space of transhumanism's confused metaphysics. All will receive the baptism offered by the new digital religions, but to ward off the evil eye, we'd best also hold fast to the integrated, decorous fabric of Burke's "ancient manners."

Let me present this book's argument formally and offer a map to what follows. My use of Przywara's diagnostic tool ranges from medieval to postmodern thinkers, as the point is to show the pattern within metaphysics that helps explain why humanism is so beleaguered. Most formally, metaphysics snaps back and forth between angelism (univocity) and vitalism (equivocity). Put in terms of political theology, it snaps back and forth between exaltation of God's sovereignty and the exorcism of this sovereignty.

Chapter 1 discusses a contemporary of Aquinas, Robert Kilwardby, who was also an outspoken critic. He argued that Thomas's theory of the metaphysical composition of singular objects falsifies the Incarnation. Aquinas's position accords far too much weight to human nature, according to Robert, who preferred to think of the divine nature of Christ as attaching to, rather than integrated with, human nature. I argue that Robert's criticism of Thomas stems from his political theology, a desire to exalt God's sovereignty in the face of a rising humanism. In Przywara's terms, Kilwardby's angelism puts emphasis on the head, and, similar to Augustine, he is in Parmenides's univocal corner. Angelism is an overemphasis, however, and thus we would also expect to see equivocity in Kilwardby. And sure enough we do. Kilwardby is most famous for his support of the plurality of forms thesis, an account of human composition that radicalizes the human into many fracturing parts. It is precisely for this reason that the divinity of Christ must attach to, but not be integrated with, human nature: an overintimacy would render Christ fragile to an unseemly degree.

In chapter 2, I argue that Robert was part of a rising tide of Augustinianism that blossomed into a complete angelism in one of the more curious questions of the Middle Ages: Can the disembodied souls of the damned nonetheless feel the physical fires of hell? Again, there is an emphasis on the head, with God's sovereignty—in this case his writ of justice—unrestrained by the fact that without bodies the damned ought not to be able to have sensations.

Chapter 3 posits that though it was a true metaphysical curiosity, the debate over hellfire and disembodied sensation not only had a long medieval life but shaped the development of early modernity. In my opinion, Descartes's *Meditations* is the most complete and arresting metaphysical work, and angelism is the center of its most famous arguments. Reid and Schopenhauer both reacted to its legacy. Schopenhauer recoiled from the vision of the human as a "winged cherub without a body," but his own thought spins uncontrollably between angelism and vitalism. Will takes the place of God, and the will's sovereignty is total (univocity) yet splintering (equivocity). Civilization is a consequence of this splintering, but discernment and ornamentation rely on division, which is suffering; evil is overcome with the ushering in of reprimitivism, once the will returns to unity. Schopenhauer's thinking on will whips between head and body, mind and matter, thought and vitalism, and the will knows no respite because the will is at war with itself.

Schopenhauer's thinking evolved from engagement with Reid, and I argue that the Scotsman's theory of natural language is a crucial insight into the unity of body and value intuition. I expand on this idea in chapters 6 through 8, but chapter 4 shows how a German tradition of biocentrism (body no head), dating back at least to elements in Schopenhauer, offered a platform for National Socialist vitalism: a blood tribalism (vitalism) offered as a critique of bourgeois civilization and its long heritage in Western institutions and manners. Establishment subverted, "Nordic cells" had their epiphany in the law of a singular mind, the führer (univocity). This decapitation replaced God with race.

Chapter 5 deals with how angels divide postmodern theorists. The Italian anarchist Agamben (b. 1942) argues that the modern managerial state is a secularization of the political theology of angelic governance crafted in the Middle Ages. The goal of his philosophy is to exorcize the "good" angels and make a full-throated return to vitalism. The American pragmatist D. G. Leahy (1937–2012) counters that the human body is best thought of as angelic greeting. A full-throated angelism best secures humanism, in fact. Both think vanity and clothes are morally worrisome. Fashion for Agamben is a continuance of angelic government, whereas for Leahy, it is a building up of self that restricts the body's angelic offering. I show how adornment and clothes to the contrary express the *analogia entis*.

Merleau-Ponty's account of flesh reiterates Thomas Reid's insight into natural language. Chapter 6 shows that flesh is the gestural body responsive to value tones or, put differently, the writ of establishment. What at first seems strange about Merleau-Ponty's phenomenology of the flesh, its frequent running together of flesh and clothes, in fact points to natural law and what Wojtyla calls the "anticipatory signs" of law in the body.

Przywara's "posture of distance" is shown to be a handy way to think of natural law. Chapter 7 presses the argument that the body is the rule of law because it is responsive to value tones that are housed in establishment. A lengthy discussion of idolatry shows that establishment is Christoform. Natural law's other name, the law of liberty, picks up on the latitude that is allowed for play and curtails the role of the state in favor of self-regulating games that are expressed in dress up, ritual, and liturgy. Clothes have, therefore, the "in-and-beyond" structure of the *analogia entis,* and time is spent in this chapter exploring what natural law can tolerate.

Chapter 8 takes its lead from Huizinga's insight that play is vitalism shot through with aesthetic and decorous value tones. It is the body always already taken up into civilization: theologically, the Incarnation. *Analogia entis* is the metaphysics of morals that avoids decapitation and natural law expressed in games, and liturgy suspends persons between vitalism and angelism. A portrait of James Bond is offered as a summary of this account of natural law as play and establishment. Finally, I return to Kilwardby's worry that the humanism underwriting the Gregorian Reform is presumption, but I conclude that inclination lifted by liturgy is, at the last, obedience to value tones, the "ultra things" of the veil of God.

Let us begin.

CHAPTER ONE

ROBERT KILWARDBY'S ANGELISM

Poor Robert. Despite his having held the Dominican Chair of Theology at Oxford, and been the archbishop of Canterbury, his intellectual standing today is not terribly high. He had the misfortune perhaps to be the contemporary of Aquinas, Bonaventure, Albert, Giles of Rome, and Peter John Olivi, to name a few of the towering intellects of the second half of the thirteenth century. Yet his somehow stodgy reputation seems to extend beyond the company he kept. Martin, for example, apparently thinks Robert didn't fully grasp Aristotle's innovations.[1] A common view is expressed by Callus, who thinks Robert was a bit befuddled by the speed of intellectual change about him.[2] Even a sympathetic commentator like fellow Dominican Richard Schenk remarks that Robert's books were not especially influential and that Robert is best viewed as a lucid witness to the ideas churning around him.[3] Schenk also makes the following argument. Robert famously documented his distance from Thomas in his philosophical letter to the archbishop of Corinth Peter Conflans. Conflans wrote to Robert demanding an explanation for his action in 1277 at the University of Oxford. Robert, with the faculty at the university,[4] condemned thirty intellectual propositions, and those concerning metaphysical composition were perceived at the time as an attack on Aquinas. This provoked intense debate, and European Dominicans (like Conflans) responded immediately and negatively[5] to the English[6] action against Aquinas.[7] According to Schenk, it was this fallout that marked Robert's greatest significance: the brouhaha created Thomism as a school of thought, one to which this present work contributes.[8] In these accounts, Robert is a bit player in the tremendous intellectual change of the period.

I am not so sure. My thesis is that Robert was an aggressive Augustinian, and a consequence of his role in 1277 was the acceleration of an Augustinian philosophy that contributed to the development of early modern angelism. Rather than being considered a conservative reactionary,[9] he is best thought of as a revivalist, someone who reignited Augustine's idealist philosophy. Viewed in this light, his 1277 intervention was a complete success. He pressed his case in his books, as well. These are full of subtlety,[10] not least his account of metaphysical composition. Employed in his treatment of the Incarnation, Robert's theory of the metaphysical composition of singulars secured an idealist treatment of Christ—"Jesus Christ is true God and true Man" (*Catechism of the Catholic Church*, para. 464)—but he decapitated the "true Man." Robert's theory of the Incarnation was one part of a broadly moving arc of Augustinianism that birthed the early modern view of the human as a "winged cherub without a body" (Schopenhauer). That Robert's life and ideas were messily involved in church power should not surprise. The real contention was political theology.

Philippe Nemo argues that the West's sui generis character derives from five distinct cultural formations.[11] Some of these are unsurprising: Greek ideas of democracy, Roman rule of law, and Jerusalem's historical consciousness and thirst for justice. What he calls the papal revolution may surprise, however. The coinage, and even the idea, is not original to Nemo but belongs to law historian Harold Berman.[12] Berman and Nemo claim that Gregory VII headed a revolutionary papal party, which, because it wanted to make earth worthy of Christ, set about reshaping Europe's governing institutions. As was not the case with the otherworldliness of Augustine's theology, which emphasized grace rather than nature in moral life, the Gregorian Reform (circa 1050–80) sought a theology that affirmed natural order and put great weight on human action and its ability to impact the world (*AE*, 248–59). In his magisterial work on the development of Western law, Berman sees Gregory as a true revolutionary, who established rule of law, constitutional principles, procedures for trial, and a criminal law sensitive to moral psychology.[13] He was also a revolutionary in the strong sense that Gregory did not shy away from using military means and alliances to impose the new order.

Nemo broadens Berman's seminal work. He is most interested in the theological framework. The grandeur and austerity of Augustine's theology of grace—"Seek not to leap off from the wood of Christ!" (*AE*, 518)—had the effect of dwarfing European innovation, contends Nemo, at least until a sort of despair gripped the church. The antidote for this despair, argues Nemo, is found in Anselmian humanism. Nemo places weight on Anselm's soteriology as the theological premise of the papal revolution. For Anselm, when the Incarnation culminated in the crucifixion, Christ gained infinite merit: this merit abolished the penalty of original sin, a sin that had cast an infinite divide between humans and God. Crucially, Christ accomplished this as Jesus, as a human: therewith, human conduct took on a radical, revolutionary, new significance; every human agent was able to reaffirm or diminish unity with God.[14] With this humanistic transformation in theology (*AE*, 508), the stage was set for Gregory's turn to Roman civil law, which he infused with biblical ethics. The effect was dramatic: the West began to emerge as a world civilization of enormous prowess.[15]

The political theology rooting this humanism in the West shows up in questions posed to Robert and Thomas by the general of the Dominicans Jean de Verceil. Gregory died in 1085, but as late as 1271, de Verceil asked Robert and Thomas questions like whether a worker is able to move hand to mallet without the angelic ministry of the celestial bodies.[16] Chenu observes that Thomas could barely disguise his disdain for such questions.[17] Thomas's reaction surely had much to do with his internalization of Gregory's project, but Verceil's request proved the staying power of the idea of angelic governance.

Did Robert favor the new humanism? There is no obvious reason to think that Robert would have just signed off on Gregory's legacy and his efforts to orient Western sensibility toward human assertion and governance. Did not Gregory ignore Augustine's warning about the "sinister part" of the world (*AE*, 516)? Not only was de Verceil perplexed in the thirteenth century but the chancellor of the University of Paris Jean Gerson was still perplexed in the fifteenth.[18] Surely, a thousand years on the matter is now *res adjudicata*? If anything, the matter is less settled: when

Gregory VII's humanism settled into the calm confidence of a Shaftesbury, it is easy to see why theologians might have been horrified. Karl
Barth, a theologian who was once on the cover of *Time* magazine, argued
that without God's revelation in Christ as waker of the dead, human
agency, even human knowing, cannot be anything but sinful.[19] Barth was
no champion of the Gregorian Reform.[20]

Przywara argues that the Fourth Lateran Council structured Thomas's
thinking, and Thomas is equally emblematic of the Gregorian revolution.
He formulated the core axiom of Christian humanism: grace perfects nature, or there is continuity between natural and supernatural goods. For if
these are foreign to one another, Thomas feared, there would be a strain on
our very idea of the good, never mind our sense of the meaning of creation
and divine providence. Robert is often billed as the "chief" of the Augustinian movement in the latter part of the thirteenth century.[21] In the common account of 1277, he plays the "heavy." Anxious about the spread of an
Arab-inflected Aristotelian naturalism, he used church authority to stamp
it out.[22] At the time, oddly enough, Robert was a well-regarded interpreter
of Aristotle, but he was not about to befriend the "more modern and progressive Aristotelianism" then afoot.[23] There is truth in this, but Robert's
action served just as much his political theology. It was a spur to Augustinianism and a dissent from *Christian* naturalism. Indeed, in Robert's case,
the conflict with humanism had been a long time coming.

As early as 1250, Robert was relying on Augustine's *De musica* and,
like Bonaventure,[24] was a proponent of the metaphysical role of music.[25]
In this, Robert stands in the normative tradition of Christian theology.
Erik Peterson explains: "Between the movement of the spheres and their
resounding, there exists an inner connection analogous to that between
the standing of the angels and their singing. . . . It is clear that all different specifications of being that focus on the cosmos, the angel, and humanity, likewise contain musical specifications. . . . The entire universe is
borne along by the song of praise."[26] The wonder is that the role of music
is absent from Thomas's metaphysics.[27] It is interesting that Przywara
forcefully corrects this omission throughout *Analogia Entis* (158–59,
314, to give a few examples).[28]

Augustine's idealism has two prongs, the epistemological and the
metaphysical, which combine to deliver the existential worry that pervades

his thinking. Przywara dubs Augustine's existential Christianity a "theology of the Cross" (see, for example, *AE,* 369, 517–18). Robert adopts Augustine's thesis that the soul is an active, not receptive, knowing power;[29] this pushes perception toward occasionalism and idealism (fully on display in Olivi's noetics, which I discuss in the next chapter). Robert's metaphysics seesaws. In thinking of natural philosophy as *musica mundana,* Robert reaffirms Augustine's Platonic idealism, which views harmonics (*numerus harmonicus*) as the deep explanation of natural phenomena (univocity). However, Augustine's signature thesis is an existential Christianity, in which a fraught history takes precedence over the serenity of natural order. Its history is fraught because natural beings are unmoored: their deepest identity is lodged not in themselves but in a transcendent musical ground,[30] and knowledge is not a communication from nature to the soul (equivocity).[31]

This equivocity finds voice in Kilwardby's relentless insistence on the plurality of forms within singular objects. Aquinas rejected this position, and Robert criticizes Thomas on metaphysical composition in the very strongest terms of subversion of the faith. The plurality-of-forms thesis intensifies the fragility of the created order, and Robert starkly contrasts its vulnerability to division (equivocity) with the integrity and unity of the godhead (univocity).[32] It is little wonder, then, that Robert casts the incarnate Word as surfing the tribulations of human life. His theory of the metaphysical composition of singulars cleverly serves his sense both that human nature is fractured and that there is a metaphysical buffer between the person of Christ and Christ's human nature.

Christ's Passion engages a conceptual knot: the intricacies of sensibility, body, and matter. Aquinas minimized the metaphysical standing of matter. He denied it was a thing (*res*), essence, act, or form.[33] By contrast, Robert considered matter a *res simplex,* essence (*aliquid habet essentiae*),[34] and substance.[35] An advocate of the *ratio seminalis,* he argued that potencies precede higher-act formations in time and by nature.[36] His plurality-of-forms thesis posits that lower forms are things used as building blocks for higher, more sophisticated creatures. This ramps up the ontological standing of the internal principles of creatures. Thomas was unusual in rejecting this thesis, arguing instead that the order of priority goes from higher act to lower. His unicity thesis maintains that each creature is one act, thing, essence, form, and this one substantial form diversifies as the acts of all a creature's powers. Robert begs to differ. For example, rather than considering the rational soul as operating as an active organizing principle of embodiment, Robert prefers to rely on a medical idea of the period,[37] the *spiritus corporeus*, a bridging phenomenon more corporal than spiritual.[38] Whether Thomas or Robert was right became one of the most hotly disputed questions of the Middle Ages.

On the back of this metaphysical difference, Robert dismisses Thomas's analysis of Christ's Passion. He holds that the happiness of Christ was the same before and after resurrection (III *Sent.* q. 46, ll. 58–61, pp. 196; ll. 613–14, p. 215). Therefore, when Jesus experienced fear, doubt, and sorrow in the Garden of Gethsemane, the emotional and appetitive part of Christ's nature was affected but not his core rationality (III *Sent.* q. 46, ll. 111–14, p. 198; ll. 200–202, p. 201). Robert reports Thomas as saying otherwise: Christ suffered thoroughly, in his reason (*quod patitur tota ratio et totaliter*) and his passions (III *Sent.* q. 46, ll. 600–603, p. 214). Robert is right: Thomas's unicity thesis compels him to argue that the suffering in the garden registered throughout Christ (*ST* III, q. 46, aa. 7–8). Thomas argues that though all the faculties of Jesus suffered on the cross, his passions did not deflect the Son's will and reason from fidelity to the Father (*ST* III, q. 46, a. 7, ad. 3).

Contrarywise, Robert's treatment of the Passion is of a piece with his plurality-of-forms thesis. Just as blood and bones have forms of their own, so is Christ's human nature layered. Christ's human nature has an integrity *in addition to* Christ's divine nature, for Christ's rational soul embossed by the Word is not "firstly and as such the life of the heart and all the other organs of the body" (primo et per se vita cordis et omnino organi corporis).[39] This layering gives a buffer, whereby the Word surfs human nature instead of being implicated in its historical fate: "There reason commanded throughout the powers of sensuality, itself remaining serenely with God" (Imperavit enim ibi ratio per omnia sensualitati, ipsa manens in dispositione sua placida et tranquilla apud Deum; III *Sent.* q. 46, ll. 628–29, p. 215). This view tends toward angelism, and its intuitive appeal is clear: it is hard to believe that the Word, God's very own self-knowledge,[40] suffered in the garden.

In a striking formulation, Robert defines a person as an "atom" in the genus of rational nature. He writes, "It is evident what is understood here by nature, namely, an individual nature in the genus of human, and by person, namely, a thing in act of singular genus remaining distinctly apart from all others" (III *Sent.* q. 8, ll. 108–9, p. 39; Ex his patet quod ad verum esse personae oportet quod sit rationalis natura. Item, quod sit atoma in illo genere).[41] A person is a thing unto itself in a high order of act (*res in actu sui generis*). With this phrasing, Robert captures wonderfully our modern sense of the otherness of each person, but how does the "atom" of the person relate to human nature? As a genus, human nature is a matter-form composite, a singular incomplete act. It is a *res* supplemented by the *res* that is the person; a person is an intensity of act crafting its own genus and is unable to suffer further supplementation. A person is the culmination of an already partially formed, partially in act, "individual" human nature, which functions as a *principium materiale* (equivocity).[42]

Wrestling against this equivocity, Robert deploys delicate language to explain the individuation of singular objects of many hefty ontological parts. A culminating form delivers a *signatio actio* making an *ens actuale et individuum*. Form unites with matter as a coparty (*coadunat et continent;* II *Sent.* q. 17, ll. 99–106, p. 64).[43] The composite *qua* form individuates the composite as an individual, and the same composite *qua* matter partially, but significantly, contracts the form to individual status. As coparties of the composite, matter and form help realize the *actualis existentia* of the composite: a term used to capture the presence of the composite's standing in individuated reality.

Though an intensity of act, a person still needs the other individuating principles of being to be adequately individuated. There is no real distinction of persons from their individuating conditions in the singular common natures, which are coparties to their identities. For Robert, individuation of persons is, one might say, a communicative phenomenon: a unity of singularizing arcs of being with an emphasis on a kernel of ontological uniqueness that is the person.

Robert's cunning treatment of the restrained fracturing of singular objects gets another loosening of the nut in the case of Christ. Robert wants to defend the claim that the happiness of Christ was the same before and after the resurrection. He needs to secure an aloofness from the trauma of human nature. Trauma? Yes: division and corruption are structural in the created order (II *Sent.* q. 20, ll. 6–11, p. 79): "omnia componibilia secundum quod huiusmodi aliquid imperfectionis habent" (III *Sent.* q. 14, ll. 7–8, p. 67). Christ transcends this structural imperfection both in person and in nature: "Persona divina est natura divina quoad identitatem. Sed illa est simplicissima" (III *Sent.* q. 14, ll. 4–5, p. 67). About natural singular objects, Robert can cogently argue that, even though the components are *res,* there is nevertheless no real distinction between nature and person on account of the *coesse* of the multiple individuating parts of the singular object (III *Sent.* q. 11, ll. 86–90, p. 58). In Christ, however, there is a real distinction between human nature and person. Christ's individuation as a person is prior to any role played by human nature (III *Sent.* q. 11, ll. 91–92, p. 58); for the person of Christ, individuated bodily, does not draw on any source of being other than the divine nature he always is.[44] Hence Christ is not a *persona composita*, as Robert puts it, but a *persona simplex*.[45] Put another way, for Robert, we have thoroughly embodied personalities, but Christ does not. As Przywara notes, Aquinas precisely tries to finesse this point (*AE*, 304–5).[46] Any treatment of the Incarnation is bound to be horribly fraught: Leo Strauss quips somewhere that Christianity drives philosophy to madness. Robert's account minimizes the humanity of Christ, and Thomas is at the other pole risking naturalizing Christ. Robert edges toward angelism, while Thomas's talk of the Incarnate Word having an *esse secundarium* through human nature moves dramatically the other way. Robert has no truck with the composition suggested by Thomas's *esse secundarium*. For Robert, the Incarnation is thus utterly gratuitous: a thoroughly historical initiative congruent with Robert's metaphysical and political dislike of naturalism.

This is not the thinking of a befuddled mind. It is best to think of Robert as kin to those Augustinians down through the centuries who have been skeptical of Aristotle's naturalism: Olivi, Malebranche, Pascal, Scheler, and even Kolnai. Kilwardby's theory of metaphysical composition is indicative of the rising tide of Augustinianism that actually reached its high-water mark in the early modern period. It should be no surprise that his angelism ends up working against his overall goal. Flipping between a musical Platonism (univocity) and a medical naturalism (equivocity)—leading to an account of the Incarnation, wherein an aloof Christ (univocity) surfs the suffering of a fracturing human nature (equivocity)—Robert's position is unstable. His aloof Christ is meant to curb Anselmian humanism, to, so to say, put humans in their proper place. With an ironic twist on the declaration of *Gaudium et Spes* (para. 22) that Christ "fully reveals man to himself," Robert's account of the Incarnation elevates an embodied Jesus to an angelic Christ. With little tinkering, one arrives at Descartes's ego, perplexed to find itself a "winged cherub without a body." In Robert's hands, Augustine's idealist philosophy is a sobering dissent from Gregory's political theology, contributing to an early modern angelism that ironically makes man a master of nature.

CHAPTER TWO

HELLFIRE AND THE BURNING FLESH OF THE DISEMBODIED

In 1270, Étienne Tempier, the bishop of Paris, condemned the proposition that the disembodied souls of the damned do not feel physical fire.[1] He reiterated the point in 1277, when condemning the proposition that disembodied souls suffering physical fire is not explainable philosophically, though by faith one might believe this.[2]

It seems the bishop of Paris had backed a losing horse. Surely, sensation without a body is a nonstarter. Are not sensations a boundary experience, occurring at the frontier where body interacts with the surrounding world? Further, do not sensations register as being on the body, about the body, or expressive of where the body is? What's true of sensations generally seems very true of touch. How can we be touched by physical fire if we have no expanse of flesh on which sensations register?[3] Surely any serious account of the integrity of nature would acknowledge that the body is written into the very idea of sensation. However, if Bishop Tempier backed a losing horse, this opens up a serious problem for the church: If, before the general resurrection of all at the end of days, the damned have no bodies, what does it matter that fire rages about them in hell? The problem, as Franciscan theologian and political theorist Peter John Olivi (1248–98) pointed out, is fundamentally one of political theology.

Few medieval theologians are darlings of the Left, but Olivi is much heralded by Europe's leading philosopher, the anarchist Giorgio

Agamben.[4] There is an irony here. Despite the philosophical conundrum, the bishop was likely serene. Saints Augustine and Gregory defended the idea of disembodied sensation, and Jesus himself spoke of the parched rich man in hell, who appealed to Abraham to let Lazarus bring him water: "for I am tormented in this flame" (Lk. 16:24).[5] Saint Ambrose had insisted that this was no mere parable: Jesus was narrating an event of disembodied desiccation. And theologians of the stature of Giles of Rome and Olivi rallied in support.

Stepping on the toes of the anarchist somewhat, Olivi argued that unless people are assured that the flames of hell await them, sin will have an intolerable liberty (*haberet intollerabilem libertatem*). God's justice requires that who sins most is most gravely punished: "It is required that who sins against the highest good is punished with the most vile and harsh penalties" (Decens enim est quod qui peccavit in summum bonum, puniatur in villissimis et acerbissimis penis).[6] To Olivi's mind, at stake is God's very sovereignty.

Is there a way to protect both God's sovereignty and the integrity of nature? Aquinas's axiom—grace perfects nature—cunningly links both. However, the agility of the axiom is not total, and Thomas denies that souls separated from their bodies can experience desiccation.[7] Disembodied desiccation would require Thomas to suspend the doctrine of secondary causes—that creatures have a natural autonomy and efficacy. As Przywara makes plain (*AE*, 292–93, 304–6), this doctrine is essential to Thomas's concept of the sacral universe, wherein creatures are causes comparable to God (*analogia entis*). Aquinas taught in Paris for two years after Tempier's intervention, solving the bishop's riddle by arguing that the damned suffer hellfire, for it is akin to a prison: flames surround the separated soul's will and block its movement. Thomas's answer poses a number of metaphysical riddles itself, but it remains true to the doctrine of secondary causes. Aquinas's account is built around humiliation: something physical (fire) controls something nobler (the spiritual will). Crucially, the will acts and is thwarted: put differently, a secondary cause does exercise its autonomous power, only impotently.

Aquinas's solution is ingenious, but just as Kilwardby was unimpressed by Aquinas's unicity-of-form thesis, so others were just as unimpressed by this humiliation thesis. The metaphysical inversion of the physical controlling the spiritual registers psychologically as humiliation and indignity, but Tempier's demand was otherwise: hellfire must register as sensation. Giles of Rome squares up to the challenge, seeking to explain how separated souls truly suffer from hellfire (*possunt vere pati ab igne inferni*) and feel themselves burning (*sentiunt se cremari*): "That amongst the damned and demons the intellect is occupied with sensation: and that such substances are burnt, because they perceive, that is, they feel themselves to be burnt."[8] Giles is explicit that "suffer" must mean to feel the impression made by fire (*sentire impressionem factam ab igne*).[9] Wanting to avoid metaphysical decapitation, Thomas balks at the idea, and thus a staple of the Franciscan *Correctorium* (a literature devoted to pointing out Thomas's errors!) is to dwell on Thomas's shyness about disembodied sensation.[10] Having sat in on the lectures of Bonaventure, and been known to have read the *Correctorium* closely,[11] Olivi positively rails against Thomas's evasion (*QN*, 151–53), not hesitating to conclude that it is dangerous, is ridiculous, and has no connection to the Catholic faith.

Underlying Thomas's naturalism is his commitment to the 1215 doctrine of the *analogia entis*. As seen in the previous chapter, there are theological intuitions that recoil from its assumed humanism, and Augustinian idealism offered a potent platform for those of Thomas's contemporaries who wanted to dissent. And dissent in numbers they did. Aquinas's most talented student, the brilliant and prolific Giles of Rome (1247–1316), pushed an angelism still found as late as Malebranche, and Jean Capreolus (1380–1444), otherwise known as the "Prince of Thomists," adopted the student's account of disembodied sensation, not the master's. As late as the 1420s, Capreolus pointedly did so to bring Thomas in line with Tempier.

Giles and Olivi argue that sensations are not causally lodged in the body but in the mind: sensation can forgo a *normal* constituent of the experience of suffering physical fire, the body, and still in no way forgo the *essential* causality of the experience. The decapitation wrought by Giles is pronounced, but Olivi radicalizes it.

Giles delivers the sovereign writ of God's justice by arguing that a sensation is essentially a mental act (univocity). It might be true, contingently, that sensations are linked with bodies, but there is no necessary connection (Saul Kripke famously reintroduced this argument to philosophy in the 1980s). Giles believed that compliance with the Parisian condemnations required that the separated souls of the damned experience hellfire as the burning of their flesh. He thus developed a metaphysics supplemented by a phenomenology in which sensations are essentially mental acts that are experienced as though they were located in an expanse of flesh—all in the absence of a body. Olivi promptly radicalized this by asserting that sensations are mental acts having no formal requirement to register in experience as spatially located: sensations are aesthetic discordances, needing neither body nor flesh to register. Their angelism consists in the claim that disembodied sensation is not unnatural: the natural, created state of man is properly mental, with no necessary connection to vitalism (univocity).

Przywara predicts that such a metaphysical emphasis will have in its wake equivocity, and sure enough Giles and Olivi rely on occasionalism to disrupt the normal (though not essential) run of causation. In other words, no sooner have they made humans into minds, like God, than they subvert the likeness by arguing that God is a cause, but the normally constituted human is not. Neither is a thoroughgoing occasionalist, but their metaphysics, wobbling between univocity and equivocity, will blossom fully in Malebranche (1638–1715).

Giles had a pronounced Augustinian sensibility and was a member of the Augustinian Order of Hermits, so it is not too surprising that that there is a convergence between the metaphysics of Giles and Malebranche.[12] Here is the opening of Malebranche's magnum opus: "But the figures and configurations of bodies and the sensations of the soul have no necessary relation to anything external. For just as a figure is round when all the exterior parts of a body are equally distant from one of its parts called its center, independently of any external body, so all the sensations of which we are capable could subsist without their being any object outside us. Their being contains no necessary relation to the bodies that seem to cause them . . . and they are nothing but the soul modified in this or that fashion."[13] Giles did not hold with Malebranche that there is only one true cause (God) and that secondary causes are mere occasions for the action of God.[14] Malebranche adopted from Avicenna the proposition that a true cause is a necessary cause, but finite substances (material or immaterial) cannot be true causes because there is no contradiction in conceiving their effects in isolation from their operations: for example, bodies are not the causes of sensations because sensory experience and bodies can be conceived in isolation. Giles also held that sensations have no "necessary relation" with the bodies that apparently cause them. Bodies *contingently* and *partially* cause sensations: contingently and partially because essentially a sensation is an act of the soul. As sensations are metaphysically "free" of the body,[15] Giles argued that in embodied experience the soul *assists* objects in registering their "effects" on the soul. Further, disembodied experience shows, if I can put it this way, that, in principle, the assistance goes all the way down. The normally constituted human is no true secondary cause.

In the case of the punishment of the damned, God suspends the causal role of the soul in sensation, but this is not a case of the divine suspension of natural order. Rather, it is the causality of an immaterial power (the soul) being replaced by a superior immaterial power (God). The natural order retains its full integrity—it continues to work on account of an immaterial causal agent—albeit now at the behest of a superior one. Giles offers a moderated occasionalism, but it is a small step to move from this position to another: that the natural order operates on account of God's direct causality *always* (Malebranche). Giles's wobble finally tips dramatically to a strident Augustinian equivocity. Commenting on the Lazarus story, Giles says, "Granted the soul of the rich man would have no physical tongue in hell, still such kind of torment by the power of God can be caused intellectually in the separated soul as would befall him living with a tongue and sensation."[16] Giles takes up what might be called "the geography of the pain." It is unclear whether Tempier required theologians to explain that the damned experience their flesh burning, but Giles sets himself that tough nut: without a body, the damned feel an *expanse* burn, that is, their flesh; the damned see the *wound* wrought by the burning (*percipit laesionem*).[17] Can a feeling of burning be isolated from the experience of flesh burning? Is the former possible without an experience of a "territory" of pain? If not, then something like a flesh, an experience of an expanse, is required as a part of the object-content. Scheler, for one, argues that certain sensations, such as pain but not seeing, essentially show themselves in phenomenological intuition as a mode of flesh (Scheler's concept of "lived body").[18] Giles agrees with Scheler, while Olivi dispenses with body and flesh both.

For Giles, pain is essentially a mental seizing of a displeasing content-object (*perceptio immutationis intentionalis displicentis*). The content-object of the burning of the damned is an *intentio horribilis*,[19] the *vilissimum objectum*,[20] and with great phenomenological insight, Giles argues that this is on account of the object-content's excessive proportion (sed secundum immutationem intentionalem, si sit ultra proportionem debitam, causatur dolor et cruciatus).[21] Horror is an experience of disproportion in flesh.

Aurel Kolnai has provided an influential phenomenology of the content-object of horror and disgust.[22] The inner structure of these content-objects is disproportion, an experience of the biological as being out of place. Giles speaks of the *intentio horribilis* as *ultra proportionem debitam,* and we all know how horror films trade on disproportion. What Giles claims the damned experience is something akin to watching a horror film. God makes and sustains the sensation of flesh burning—generating a content-object of a burning of the body that is not really extant—and the damned react with *horror at the sight*. About the illusion of film, the Polish phenomenologist Ingarden says, "One forgets that in actuality the merely presented objectivities are not at all that which they only pretend to be."[23] Surveying contemporary explanations of the sensations of the disembodied, Olivi documents some theorists as arguing that the experience is akin to dreaming or fantasy (*quasi sensibiliter afflictivam*) (*QN* ll. 47–50, p. 150). Giles is trying to convey an experience that is similar to what we mean when we say "that makes my skin crawl," and, as we can all attest, that experience, if not real, is real and horrible *enough*.

Olivi expands Giles's suggestion that the suffering of the damned is linked to aesthetics. However, by adopting a forthright Augustinian idealism, Olivi intensifies decapitation, jettisoning flesh as part of a burning sensation and mentalizing aesthetic experience.[24]

Similar to Kilwardby, Olivi is fond of Augustine's *De musica*. Olivi pairs the damned's aesthetic recoil from hellfire with Augustine's argument that a song strikes us as discordant when the music is out of proportion with our emotional register. How good is the analogy? Even if in the two cases there is an internal emotional reaction, the music example still relies on vibrations registering in the body to which our emotions then react. However, this way of thinking—external objects registering with the spirit and compelling internal reactions—is wrong, according to Olivi's lights. Spirit is an active epistemological power, a permanent openness to the world—something like an absorbing psychological gauze spread out onto the world, but one that is able to hone in on particular objects of attention. Olivi termed this intentionality *aspectus* and those objects that become the object-contents of intentional consciousness *terminative causes*—that is, the object is the spot where self-actualizing mental perceptions arrive, not where they start.[25] Spirit *expresses* the object in its intentionality (*similitudo et sigillaris expressio*). This is what a sensation properly is.[26]

Olivi actually has nothing to explain about how the "jump" happens between hellfire and spirit without a mediating sensuous flesh. That humans have such a flesh in our ordinary sublunar state is always accidental to our actually having sensations (*QN* ll. 441–43, p. 163). Nothing special happens to the disembodied because we are always, even as embodied, more akin to angels anyway. His angelism is a divinization of man and thus pushes Olivi toward univocity. Przywara predicts a wobble, and sure enough angels are most curious creatures in Olvi's telling. True angels relate to one another in certain quasi-physical ways (equivocity). Olivi seems to think of the good angels as a press gang. In the age of sail, the Royal Navy had the authority to send crews into towns to forcibly conscript new crewmembers. The good angels, Olivi tells us, register their own power in demons by means of a touching or constraining pressure in spiritual space (*per viam efficacie tactive seu inpressive*); otherwise, they could not detain demons or torture them painfully (*alias boni angeli non possent demoni violenter detinere aut movere aut afflictive torquere*).[27] Angels, he says, move in two ways. The first is by moving place and "the other is by keenness and a virtual range of sight, or the intentions of their powers, here and there spread forth or directed to diverse objects, just as is experienced in us, not only when we are stirred [by the will] to various acts of perception and seeing, but also when beginning to daydream we experience the intentions of the inner and outer senses drawing back to the interior and then amidst the excitement [of the dream] we experience the intentions virtually spreading out to the exterior. And this Augustine teaches both in *On Genesis* 12 and in his book *On the Trinity.*"[28] Fantasy is offered here as a model for a full-blown idealism and shifts sensation significantly to the mental. Olivi links this model to two other elements of Augustine's epistemology, one derived from *City of God* and the other from *De musica.*

Four concurrent causes join to make up the suffering of the damned: the suitability or proportionality of the object (fire), the divine power that binds the soul and its object, the aesthetic rule of the soul, and the impotence of the will (*QN* ll. 366–71, p. 161).

According to Augustine's *City of God,* pain is what opposes our will (*dissensus voluntatis*) (an axiom in Schopenhauer's philosophy). Olivi explicitly rejects Avicenna's definition of pain—pain is the division of parts of the body—arguing this definition is correct enough for those things with bodies (vitalism), but Augustine's definition, being more formal and universal, is far preferable (*QN,* 149, 163) (univocity). According to Augustine's *De Musica,* sensibility is ordered by an aesthetico-emotional rule of proportionality (*complantata affectio proportionalium*) that is the basis of our love of objects (cf. Max Scheler on the *Ordo Amoris*). Sensation is never raw, therefore, but always under emotional, aesthetic judgment. This principle of judgment diversifies and channels our acts of will. Objects contrary to this rule are thus contrary to our will and are painful and provoke hatred. God inserts as a punishment an emotional rule into the separated souls of the damned, such that hellfire is disproportionate (*affectio proportionis contrarie ad proportionem seu improportionalitatem ardoris infernalis*). Spirits always have an emotional rule so the penal emotional dynamic inserted by God is thus a naturally functioning power (*quia ita est sibi inserta ac si ab initio fuisset sibi connaturalis*) and is permanently painful because it is contrary to the will (*resultat dolor intensissimus et quasi connaturalis effectus*).

It need not be this way. God implants into the damned an emotional register that hates fire, but God can insert a different aesthetic range that would not be similarly adversely affected by fire. My mind leaps at once to *Game of Thrones* and the dragon queen, Daenerys Targaryen, but Olivi is surely thinking of Exodus 3:2: "And the angel of the Lord appeared unto him in a flame of fire out of the midst of a bush."

In Giles, the damned react in horror at the sight of their wounded flesh. Olivi interiorizes this experience, arguing the damned suffer through their hatred of hellfire. This experience is not provoked by a change in the body or the flesh (Scheler's "lived body") but is part of the soul's mental furniture: the aesthetic-emotional standard of judgment all souls contain. It is in God's power to change the character of this principle. Objects, being neutral, are "terminative causes": their value tones reaching them, so to say, from this "subjective" aesthetic sense. Here, realism gives way to an occasionalist idealism.

Olivi was quick to see that Anselmian humanism was a threat to God's sovereignty. Aquinas exemplified this by so wedding human nature to the body that in its absence hell became a prison rather than a torture chamber. To Olivi's eyes, Thomas's commitment to secondary causality constrains God to deliver an eternity not of hate and horror but of humiliation. As we saw at the start of the chapter, for Olivi, strict justice requires more. Curiously, to deliver this justice, Olivi's angelism divinizes the damned.

CHAPTER THREE

EARLY MODERN ANGELISM
AND SCHOPENHAUER'S VITALISM

In *The World as Will and Representation*, Schopenhauer makes an astute observation. In 1818, he seeks a course correction. Revisiting the development of modern philosophy from Descartes to Berkeley and up to Kant, Schopenhauer identifies, and wants to block, the prevailing idea that the knowing subject is "a winged cherub without a body."[1] Schopenhauer, is, I think, correct: angelism is a fair summation of the philosophical doctrine wrought by the introduction of Descartes's idealism.[2]

It was by no means new, however. Our first two chapters discussed the use theologians made of Augustinian idealism to counter Thomistic naturalism, which counted among its sources Anselm, Gregory VII, and the Fourth Lateran Council. The cost of this riposte was decapitation. Robert Kilwardby's account of the Incarnation offered a vision of man, wherein personhood stands aloof from nature. Giles of Rome and Peter John Olivi gave a boost to this angelism with their arguments to show that sensations do not require movements of physical organs. A sensation is a mental seizing of an object-content: the soul is a total cause of perception, with the sensed object having no more than an occasionalist standing.

Descartes, Leibnitz, Malebranche, Berkeley, Hume, and Thomas Reid all think disembodied sensation is possible, and some of them even think it as normative. Reid found Berkeley's idealism not easily answerable: "Nor can any man shew, by any good argument" writes Reid, "that all our sensations might not have been as they are, though no body, nor quality of body, had ever existed."[3] In Berkeley, angelism is full-blown:[4] the only things that exist are minds and mental events. For him, flesh, objects, and the world are all interconnections among ideas. Berkeley's arguments are ingenious, but Descartes is in the background, and the scholastic debate haunts his opening meditations: "I will imagine that the sky, air, earth, colours, shapes, sounds and everything external to me are nothing more than the creatures of dreams by means of which an evil spirit entraps my credulity. I shall imagine myself as if I had no hands, no eyes, no flesh, no blood, no senses at all, but as if my belief in all these things were false."[5] Modern idealism owes much to its medieval parent. Though Schopenhauer rejects the idea of the knowing subject as a "winged cherub without a body," his whole philosophy has an uncanny similarity to these scholastic debates. Consider that in Olivi's account, God surrounds the damned with flames. Unable to halt the experience of the flames, the emotion of hatred (*affectio detestativa*) floods the soul and triggers a forlorn effort on the part of the damned to be rid of the fire. The knowing subject is similarly afflicted in Schopenhauer. The will surges in consciousness, and its manifestations afflict the person, who, lacerated by the torments of the will, seeks refuge in aesthetic experience and escape in self-renunciation. The effort is futile, for though the self might slip away, its very dissolution is fodder for the will's ever-renewing mortification. The self will be rebuilt, albeit under different conditions of identity, and once more be afflicted by the will that it perversely fed during its own escape. Alert to the problem of decapitation, Schopenhauer's metaphysics nonetheless snaps back and forth between univocity and equivocity, with a final emphasis on vitalism.

Yet how can the self ever stand at sufficient distance from the will to separate itself from the will's lusts? Suddenly, in the midst of Schopenhauer's atheism, the archbishop of Canterbury Robert Kilwardby makes a cameo: personhood, pristine and aloof from a splintering nature, commands and cancels nature (*WWR*, 1:152, 411). At the last, angelism returns with a vengeance (*WWR*, 1:405) and momentarily forestalls vitalism. Here, the final emphasis is on angelism, but the whole is, as Przywara warns, a snapping back and forth between univocity (angelism) and equivocity (vitalism).

Reid and Schopenhauer were great admirers of Bishop Berkeley. Until he was about thirty years old, Reid was a convinced Berkeleyian. The first page of *The World as Will and Representation* draws to a close with Schopenhauer praising Berkeley's "immortal service to philosophy." Praise is owed, thinks Schopenhauer, for Berkeley brings to utter clarity Descartes's idea that "the world is representation" (*WWR*, 1:3). Nonetheless, both philosophers recoil from Berkeley's angelism. In a frame set by Berkeley, each seeks a refined realism (*WWR*, 1:120, 128; 2:430) and a fresh account of our embodiment. Schopenhauer also admired Reid,[6] yet described his own account as the inverse of Reid's (*WWR*, 2:186). The differences between the two will become clear, but, against Berkeley, Schopenhauer argues that an attentive phenomenology of will shows that experience is always a modification of the body (vitalism). For his part, Reid argues that Berkeley missed the crucial place of the body in language and thus experience. Adjudicating between these modified realisms, I will argue that on the substantive issue—how to counter angelism with an adequate account of the role of the body in experience—it is Reid who gets the better of the winged cherub. His account of the gestural body cunningly slips between angelism and vitalism and conforms to the *analogia entis*, offering a platform for a liturgy of morals.

The hint of trouble in Schopenhauer's own account comes with the very opening of *The World as Will and Representation*: "'The world is my representation:' this is a truth valid with reference to every living and knowing being, although man alone can bring it into reflective, abstract consciousness. If he really does so, philosophical discernment has dawned upon him. It then becomes clear and certain to him that he does not know a sun and an earth, but only an eye that sees a sun, a hand that feels an earth" (*WWR*, 1:3). So begins the philosophy book I most enjoy reading, but it is an odd start. Can the third sentence be true? Do I truly not know the sun but "only an eye that sees the sun"? Schopenhauer thinks it is true because, for him, a sensation is the striving of will embodied and phenomenologically present (*WWR*, 1:107, 152). However, in his desire to overcome Berkeley's angelism, has he overstated the role of the body (vitalism) or, in the identification of body and experience,[7] has he in fact folded the body back into the mind,[8] surreptitiously overmentalizing sensation and snapping back into an ironclad idealism (angelism)?

Unlike Schopenhauer, Reid argues that sensations are content laden because they are language bearing. Whereas Schopenhauer has the mind build experience from sensation data, Reid sees the mind as a witness to an extramental cosmos. The essential difference is Reid's theory of the gestural body: what is (the ontic) and what is known (the noetic) are internally linked in the "lived body." In fact, Reid helps us see that Scheler's "lived body" is better cast as a liturgical body. By contrast, we will see that metaphysical decapitation stalks Schopenhauer's thinking, and he never quite escapes.

In the *Meditations,* Descartes complains that while trying to think silently about sensation his mind leaps to the use of customary language: "For although I think about these things to myself, silently and without speaking, I am still restricted to these words and am almost deceived by ordinary language. For we say that we see the wax itself if it is present, not that we judge that it is there from its colour and shape. From this way of talking I might conclude immediately that the wax is therefore known by how the eye sees and not by an inspection of the mind alone."[9] Descartes's worry that language obscures perception is Berkeley's point of attack. Developing the medieval British tradition of nominalism in a highly original way, Berkeley argues that experience and language are entwined. In particular, he argues that the identity of any object given to us in sensation is secured by a name. He writes, "men combine together several ideas, apprehended by diverse senses, or by the same sense at different times, or in different circumstances but observed however to have some connexion in Nature, either with respect to co-existence or succession; all which they refer to one name, and consider as one thing."[10] Reid tells us that for a good while he was a convinced Berkeleyian. He credits Berkeley with an insight that structured all his subsequent thinking: "It is therefore a just and important observation of the Bishop of Cloyne, That the visible appearance of objects is a kind of language used by nature, to inform us of their distance, magnitude, and figure" (*IE,* 64).

Berkeley thinks that objects, space, and time, are structures of language, and though Reid is smitten with Berkeley's "language of nature" thesis, he deftly turns it away from idealism by defending the claim that perceptions are signs witnessing to extramental objects (*IE,* 43–44). Schopenhauer hints at the Berkeleyian theme when he speaks of science as being able to stand before nature only as if it were before "hieroglyphics that are not understood" (*WWR*, 1:97),[11] but he nonetheless lodges language firmly in rationality (with an important exception, music, which I discuss at the end of the chapter). He leaves this British strain of reflection on sensation and "the language of nature" fallow, which significantly hampers his effort to develop a robust but sober account of embodiment.

Reid argues that language is impossible without an intuitive grasp of the body: language is, foundationally, movement of the body. The body, an organized complex object moving in time and spread out in space, is inseparable from human experience and belief. National and technical languages build on natural language. According to Reid, "The elements of this natural language, or the signs that are naturally expressive of our thoughts, may, I think, be reduced to these three kinds: modulations of the voice, gestures, and features" (*IE*, 33). If, as Berkeley argues, language is necessary to stabilize sensations and thus constitutive of the perception of objects, then, adds Reid, perception also relies on a prior exposure to a complex object cohering in space and time, the body. Language ultimately sits atop a gestural body. Reid's model for the gestural body is the ritual of the law courts. Court, game, play, gesture, and decorum constitute the rule of law intrinsic to embodied consciousness (*analogia entis*). For this reason, Reid famously rejected all state-of-nature theory: humans cannot enter into "the compacts of civilization" because our bodies are always already ritualized as rule of law. To have a body is to have unions and agreements (*IE*, 32) (vitalism and civilization). Fatefully, despite his high regard for Berkeley and Reid, Schopenhauer does not pursue this line of inquiry into language (*WWR*, 2:165), and his thinking teeters on "reprimitivism" (Kolnai) (vitalism without civilization).

The heart of Schopenhauer's account of sensation is found in section 21 of *On the Fourfold Root*. He refers to this section frequently in both volumes of *The World as Will and Representation*. Our bodies are "through and through only concrete will, phenomenon of the will" (*WWR*, 1:405), and this great passage from *On the Fourfold Root* captures wonderfully the grasping hand of the will: "Ultimately the perceptions of sight refer to touch; indeed, vision is to be considered an imperfect, but extensive touch that makes use of light rays as long feelers" (*FR*, 55). The body here is akin to a proboscis. It is vital—"the in-itself of life," relaying data—but not yet gestural.

This is confirmed both by Schopenhauer's repeated formulations of sensations as data and his firmly lodging language in the faculty of reason. Perception is a function of the understanding and is distinct from conceptual reason (*WWR*, 1:38–39): crucially, language belongs squarely with the latter. Speech, "a very complete telegraph communicating arbitrary signs" (*WWR*, 1:39) is the first product of reason, he says, and "only by the aid of language does reason bring about its most important achievements" (*WWR*, 1:37), namely, the compacts of civilization. An exchange of concepts, language is "reason speaking to reason" (*WWR*, 1:40). Hearing is called "the sense of reason," he says, because it is the medium of language (*FR*, 55). In Schopenhauer, the body always appears under the principle of sufficient reason (understanding) and, therefore, as organized, but experience is not the language of nature made visible in the gestural body.

For Schopenhauer, the will is double in aspect, mind and body simultaneously. On the one hand, our own body is "the starting-point for each of us in the perception of the world" (*WWR*, 1:19), and Schopenhauer puts his point nicely: "it is true that space is only in my head; but empirically my head is in space" (*WWR*, 2:184). On the other hand, we have the following superb image: "Therefore the externality to us to which we refer objects, on the occasion of sensations of sight, is itself really within our heads; for that is its whole sphere of activity. Much as in the theatre we see the mountains, the woods, and the sea, but yet everything is inside the house" (*WWR*, 2:188). Fantasy, theater, court of law—Olivi, Schopenhauer, and Reid are hovering over the same ground. On the one hand, fantasy and theater put Olivi and Schopenhauer in the same idealist corner, but theater and courtroom drama seem to link Schopenhauer and Reid. But how? Reid is a metaphysical realist,[12] who believes sensations are a *witness* to discrete bodies in space and time. Realism, says Schopenhauer, "overlooks the fact that the object no longer remains object apart from its reference to the subject, and that, if one takes this away or abstracts from it, all objective existence is also immediately nullified" (*FR*, 37). Reid would conclude that Schopenhauer overlooked the possibility that, just as the will is double in aspect, so too is representation: sensations give testimony of things we indeed never directly experience. He writes, "In the testimony of nature given by the senses, as well as in human testimony given by language, things are signified to us by signs: and in one as well as the other, the mind, either by original principles or by custom, passes from the sign to the conception and belief of the things signified" (*IE*, 90). Just as in a court of law, where the witness recounts events that the jury did not and never can see, so do sensations recount events with which consciousness neither has nor can ever have a direct relationship.[13] This does not stop experience from being reportage.[14]

Reid is sure to press Schopenhauer: How different is a witness from a spectator in the theater? Schopenhauer is wily, however: the spectator is what he calls the principle of sufficient reason, and there is nothing ludic or dramatic about this principle.

A "wide gulf" exists between sensation and perception, and "the law of causality alone can bridge across this gulf" (*WWR*, 2:208). Sensations are "much too uniform and lacking in data" (*FR*, 57) to account for our perception. We never have such a thing as a "mere sensation," so how does Schopenhauer know such raw, impoverished things exist? Reid doubts he *can* know. About a very eighteenth-century ailment, his gout, Reid says, "I have not only a notion of pain, but a belief of its existence, and a belief of some disorder in my toe which occasions it; and this belief is not produced by comparing ideas, and perceiving their agreements and disagreements: it is included in the very nature of the sensation" (*IE*, 118). To make his point, Schopenhauer turns to certain puzzles in optics. Struck by the fact that in vision, twin "images" lodge one in each eye and yet we see but one object, he concludes, "that which is doubly felt through the sense is only singly perceived intuitively." Further, in vision the impression of the object is first on the retina reversed and upside down. The understanding uses its causal law to move backward from the sensation, "whereby the cause presents itself upright, externally, as an object in space" (*FR*, 59). Employing the law of causality and the forms of space and time, Schopenhauer asserts that "the understanding first creates and produces this objective world" (*FR*, 52). This generative mental law is a priori, unlearned because "physiologically, it is a function of the brain, which learns this function from experience no more than the stomach to digest or the liver to secrete bile" (*FR*, 57). It is machinelike and lacks the play and decorum of testimony at court (for Przywara on the role of play in epistemology, see *AE,* 128).

Schopenhauer is fond of medical cases. For him, the case of the seventeenth-century Cambridge don Saunderson, a man born blind, who nonetheless came to have a magnificent understanding of space, proves space is not a function of sensation but is a mental law *(FR,* 57). Even more startling is the case of Eva Lauk, who, born with no legs or arms, had a complete grasp of the world by means of sight alone, and achieved it as fast as another able-bodied child (*FR,* 57). Echoing Giles and Olivi, Schopenhauer asserts that these cases prove that "sensation merely furnishes the opportunity" to have perception, but "time, space, and causality do not come to us from the outside, neither through vision, nor through touch, but have an internal origin, and thus not an empirical, but an intellectual origin" (*FR,* 57).

Reid would reply to Schopenhauer's example of Eva with his wonderful image of an infant learning the world: the child stares at an object, playfully handling the object to come at it from all different angles and sensory vantages (*IE,* 103). Poor Eva would have come at the world in just the same way: in playing, she would have marshaled her senses, including her sense of touch from other parts of her body. Scheler credits Reid with being the first philosopher to think seriously about child epistemology and the role of play.

What of blind people who later gain their sight? These sad cases are rare, and the newly sighted seldom prosper. These patients come to see, but what they see has little coherence. Even in the Bible, when Jesus heals the blind man, the man reports, "I see men as trees, walking." The late British neurologist Oliver Sacks believed the profound difficulties encountered may result from the brain's being asked to reverse a lifetime of compensatory adaptation and specialization.[15] Patients pick up visual details but struggle to form a complex perception. Can their brains simply not apply the law of causality to vision? A strange detail has been repeated in cases across the centuries: patients have been observed holding a cat, looking intently first at an ear and then at a paw and touching each part gently. They know the cat, which coheres to touch but not in vision.[16]

For Schopenhauer, one would expect the principle of sufficient reason to kick in and bring coherence to sight. Schopenhauer might have relied on Sack's theory to explain the anomaly. The case would have equally troubled Reid. Sight should give testimony to the cat's existence. The newly sighted do exactly what the infant does: they stroke the ears of the cat, looking intently at it, but report seeing only parts of the animal. Why can they not learn like the infant? A curious fact is that the newly sighted report finding bodies ugly and the stains and blemishes on skin disgusting.[17] They avoid looking at faces, and even a year after the operation cannot recognize individual faces or facial expressions.[18] Reid might have argued that the language of nature is scrambled because the play of the newly sighted is incomplete; it is not carried along by the decorous. Recalling how scripture links play and the delightful, disgust interrupts play, keeping things out of place.

Play spans the nonhuman animal and human worlds, and thus Reid argues that for animals, idiots, and children, as well as for those of us possessing "common understanding," "the language of Nature is the universal study" (*IE*, 102). Play is always aesthetic and is thus linked to a decorous gestural body. Obedience to the rules of the games is always a part of play, and this is why Reid says that sensations are natural signs that immediately prompt beliefs about the properties of external objects (*IE*, 41).[19] Liturgy defers to objects.

Unsurprisingly, therefore, Schopenhauer believes that the mind "recasts" (*umarbeitet*) (*FR*, 54)[20] the world. Before the work of the mind, sensations are rudimentary things: not as bleak as Descartes's *res extensa* perhaps but still not the content-rich perceptions relayed by Reid. The mind must first mentalize the "raw material" of sensation: work, for Schopenhauer, is not the *artes mechanicae* that craft human objects from the integrity and resistance encountered in the world. "But now I will first more precisely demonstrate," says Schopenhauer, "the great gulf between sensation and intuition as I explain *how raw is the stuff* from which this beautiful work proceeds" (*FR*, 54; emphasis added; cf. *WWR*, 1:12; 2:167).

Reid is a challenge to Schopenhauer's claim that the perception of an object is an *achievement* of the mind organizing sensations lodged under the skin of the body. Schopenhauer thinks "I do not know the sun but only an eye that sees the sun," because he believes it is true that the human person is one "who as the condition of every object is the supporter of this whole world" (*WWR*, 1:205). The straining work of Atlas is not for Reid: for him, it is not too strong to say that perception is an obedient conduit of the world's manifestation. Sensation displays the *analogia entis* because it has the structure "in-and-beyond" (*AE*, xxii).

If, as I have argued, Schopenhauer struggles in his wrestle with the winged cherub, why did he eschew the line of inquiry inaugurated by Berkeley into language and perception? In his excellent book, Patrick Gardiner points out that Schopenhauer for years toyed with the idea of making a translation of David Hume's *Dialogues concerning Natural Religion*.[21] Schopenhauer knew that Reid was an admiring critic of Hume. He was also aware, no doubt, that Reid, like Berkeley, was a churchman.

On at least three occasions in *On the Fourfold Root*, Schopenhauer warns philosophers against their tendency toward "theological flirting" (*FR*, 40). Hume's basic argument in his *Dialogues* is that religions are intellectually unsound because they rely so heavily on testimony, absent any other means of verification. Reid's clever response is to show that all perception relies on witness, and witness is really liturgy. We are set serenely in the cosmos, calmly responsive to, and ritually reciting, its manifestation. An adequate accounting of sensation shows Reid that, as with Aquinas, we inhabit a sacral cosmos (*AE*, 271).

CHAPTER FOUR

VITALISM AND NATIONAL SOCIALISM

For Schopenhauer, the human person is, at root, "the will that is always in need of strife."[1] Civilization—opera, ballet, painting, literature, and philosophy—is the strife of the will. Civilization is not soteriology. The religious practice of chastity and asceticism is necessary: "But we now turn our glance from our own needy and perplexed nature to those who have overcome the world, in whom the will, having reached complete self-knowledge, has found itself again in everything, and then freely denied itself, and who then merely wait to see the last trace of the will vanish with the body that is animated by that trace" (*WWR,* 1:411).

It is absurd to say that Schopenhauer was a Nazi, but there is undoubtedly an avenue from *The World as Will and Representation*—unquenchable vitalism and a *final* skepticism towards civilization teetering on reprimitivism—to the metaphysics of National Socialism. Political discussions often devolve into name-calling.[2] There are lots of names to throw at political opponents: absolutist, Bonapartist, totalitarian, Stalinist, Caesarist, Communist, Ayatollah, reactionary, papist, falangist, even ultramontanist, but the two perennial favorites are undoubtedly Fascist and Nazi. For an interesting twist, I read a newspaper article, in which Islamic State of Iraq and the Levant (ISIL) fighters were described as "repressed Nazis." Although these terms are readily used, most people likely could not easily identify the primary political attributes of a Fascist. Even with regard to Nazis, people are likely to have only vague ideas about the Gestapo, death camps, Brownshirts, or the word-of-the-moment hatred.

Aurel Kolnai's 1938 *The War against the West*—described by the German social theorist Axel Honneth as "groundbreaking"—is surely the most detailed, analytical documentation of the thoughtscape of Nazism by a philosopher.[3] Nazism is a tribal egotism, argues Kolnai, simultaneously a cult of the male body (*WAW,* 82) (vitalism) and a sacralization of the state (*WAW,* 37) (angelism), and simultaneously a politics limited for a race (vitalism) and an appetite for empire expressive of the revealed law of a divinized führer (*WAW,* 29, 60) (angelism): an erotics of the same flipping back and forth with an erotics of an utterly singular ego. As expressed in 1935 by Hans Frank, imperial minister of justice, Germany's categorical imperative was to ask only "What would the führer say?" (*WAW,* 29). Race (body) and führer (mind) combined to create a monster, because Nazi political erotics relied on a series of decapitations—warping persons, family, and community, and warping them catastrophically.

Burke recommends that politics obey a "method of nature," but this is quite different from Nazi "pagan romantic vitalism."[4] The Nazis wanted nothing to do with Burke's effort to drape political passions in "the spirit of a gentleman, and the spirit of religion" and aimed instead at a root and branch remaking of society, comparable in *ambition* to the French Revolution. At issue, Kolnai contends, is not straightforwardly the open combat to come but the revolutionary assault on the value architecture of the West: its moral, political, metaphysical, and cultural convictions and tendencies are all put in dispute by National Socialism (*WAW,* 311).

To add one more peculiarity to these singularities, when looking at contemporary Western politics, it is not outlandish to observe continuities between the managerial state and Mussolini's formula for fascism: "Liberty of real man: the *liberty of the state* and of man *in* the state" (*WAW,* 124). As Kolnai points out, this chilling formulation was far outstripped by Nazism's "weird idealism of tyranny" (*WAW,* 125). It is this fetishization of tyranny, and its roots in vitalism, that marks out Nazism's ambition for "the fall of the West" and "the revival of spiritual barbarism" (*WAW,* 23).

Kolnai picked out broad topics dear to the Nazis, for example, the desire for national greatness or the eroticism of military life, and then gathered under these headings dozens and dozens of quotes from Nazi writers. Kolnai literally collected Nazi literature as it was being handed out in the streets and cafes of Vienna. Although he mostly allowed the

Nazis to speak for themselves, he also interjected commentary in *The War against the West* that expresses Kolnai's Leftist sensibility at the time. This is reflected in the book's thesis: Nazism is more anti-Western than Bolshevism and is "fundamentally opposed" to Liberalism (*WAW,* 22, 96–97); it seeks to reprimitivize a civilization.

As a convert to Catholicism, Kolnai was horrified to see Catholic intellectuals hold their noses and find common cause with Hitler (*WAW,* 258–63): many welcomed National Socialism as an anti-utilitarian, anti-liberal, and anti-Communist movement, believing that they could flush away its most poisonous aspects and ultimately redirect the movement to higher spiritual fields.[5] Kolnai warned again and again that any compromise with the Nazis by religious or political authorities would prove to be utterly foolish. It was not a revival movement, he contended, but a revolution bent on deflating civilization itself. Today, we tend to think of World War II as a matter of moral clarity, but it must be remembered that its heroes, people like Charles de Gaulle and Winston Churchill, came to power as hardliners: they were thought suspect because they were overly indifferent to the possibility of compromising with Hitler. Into the war itself, Lord Halifax and Chamberlain raised that possibility. In shades of today, some thought even more broadly that compromise and radical variety were built into the very meaning of democracy, a position Kolnai wholeheartedly rejected.

By the end of the war, Kolnai had morphed into a brilliant conservative theorist. His theoretically rich "Privilege and Liberty" appeared in 1949, but it is his provocative 1950 "Three Riders of the Apocalypse" that most pointedly takes up the themes of *The War against the West*, except now his thesis has changed significantly.[6] In 1950, Kolnai argued that the three modern mass regimes—Nazism, Communism, and Progressive democracy—were linked as a three-headed monster having a single body: "emancipated Man." Each, albeit to different degrees, was infected "by the virus of subversive utopia bound for a totalitarian goal":[7] Marxist-Leninism, though, offered "that most genuine and powerful brand of Totalitarianism."[8] Soviet totalitarianism, he thought, accepted the West's values but callously betrayed them. Communism sought to use the West's scientism to launch a pervasive, thoroughgoing transformation of nature. For this reason, Kolnai ultimately came to see Bolshevism as the more complete totalitarianism, concluding that the scientism of Communism resulted in the fullness of the human being's "self-enslavement" and outstripped even Nazism's spiritual barbarism.[9]

The "emancipation of Man" is the root doctrine of this "three-headed monster,"[10] and a clue to the meaning of this phrase appears right at the start of *WAW* in Kolnai's arresting comment that "Klages is not far from Freud" (*WAW*, 15). Ludwig Klages, described by Kolnai as a highly admired Dionysian (*WAW*, 68), was a leading advocate of vitalism, and a recurring theme in *WAW* is the Nazi reduction of personality to vitality. An advocate of decapitation, Klages writes, "Personality (Person) and Universal Nature (All) are hostile antipodes: one must eliminate the former to realize the latter" (*WAW*, 69).

The Nazis did not emerge from a vacuum: hence Kolnai's mention of vitalists like Nietzsche and Freud (*WAW*, 14). Kolnai believed that Nietzsche's talk of the nobility as persons of "high temperature" was utterly subversive. Klages took up this way of thinking in his biocentrism (*biozentrismus*): the folding of metaphysics into biology (*WAW*, 198–201), which easily lent itself to exaggeration in the race preoccupations of the Nazis and helped give them intellectual standing. They simply exploited patterns in contemporary German thought, contended Kolnai. A long and significant trend of Western thinking ended with Nazism: "Here the metaphysics of fascist counter-revolution are completed" (*WAW*, 181).

Kolnai might not have been as precocious as David Hume, but by his early twenties he was a minor figure in the Vienna Circle, having authored his first book, *Psychoanalysis and Sociology*, at age twenty-two. However, in 1925, and in the presence of Freud, he read a paper to the circle entitled "Max Scheler's Critique and Assessment of Freud's Theory of Libido." It is a definitive break with Freud, in which Kolnai argues that Freud's preoccupation with a few elemental drives undermines the deference that every civilization needs to pay to the objective order of values:

> But the phenomenological method, as its name already implies, approaches things from precisely the opposite direction from the psychoanalytical. . . . Rather than explaining, deciphering, deriving and reducing the phenomena to their common denominator, or establishing the laws of their occurrence and development, it tries to intuit and grasp their immediate

"essences" and to hold fast, through the most appropriate concepts and descriptions, all their varieties, together with their ideal, unvarying, "connections of meaning." In the last analysis, the aim of this method is not to make possible the control and manipulation of the matter being investigated for the sake of healing, but to analyse it for the sake of understanding. (*PVNS*, 1)

Civilizations exist, thought Kolnai, to ensure the refinement of human persons. Refinement requires deference to the range of moral, aesthetic, and technical values acknowledged to stand above us, not a fascination with vitalism.[11] Freud was philosophically confused: his fascinations would only stunt personality (Jung's critique of Freud is comparable to Kolnai's). Civilization makes human persons free, but civilizations tap into a complex and varied hierarchy of values: hedonic, vital, moral, intellectual, and religious.[12] "Children, though compelled to obey, are kings because they are enticed away, enchanted, into the fairyland of idealized mankind, into the innocent sphere of pure mathematics, into the abstract and leisurely world of eternal forms."[13] Emancipation from this hierarchy is not freedom but barbarity.

Burke provided Kolnai with a sexual politics. The Burkean method of nature is in "the spirit of philosophic analogy," where nature and politics both exhibit a "family settlement." In the natural world, creatures thrive by balancing inheritance, territory, and reproduction; by analogy, the soil of politics is family property, fertility in marriage, and home (vitalism), each of which are life girders that defer to value clusters—moral, aesthetic, and technical (angelism).[14] Family property intersects with the nation's guiding institutions (angelism), which have a history but which also have stable coordinates in space and time. Similar to a family, establishment has a past (history), present (place), and future (trajectory).

In consequence, Burke argued that a vigorous defense of rights depends on upholding establishment. Rights, he believed, were historically earned: there is no so-called natural right because rights are birthed with institutions of law. Revolution, he thus warned, was no great drama to be celebrated but a wrecking of institutions that leaves the people exposed to raw government power. If linked to an assault on religion, revolution becomes monstrous. A divine lawgiver foreign to and greater than the

state relativizes the reach of the state (*AE,* 182–83). Remove divine law
and state power becomes limitless, rooting out "family settlement," for
attacks on religion are invariably also attacks on property. Church property is managed for the ages, a physical reminder to government that its
power serves a social bond transcending immediate pressures: a bond of
the dead, living, and not yet born.

The Nazis rejected this sexual politics. The Nazi Männerbund was,
says Kolnai, a bond "differing at the very outset both from the natural and traditional forms of community and allegiance, such as family,
patriarchal kingship, or settled social customs—and from the rational
and contractural type of association," such as trade unions, social clubs,
and professional bodies (*WAW,* 75; *PVNS,* 47). Nazism was not built
around analogy but, celebrating "tribal self-enclosure," around a monistic vitalism, an equivocity of drives detached from the inherited markers
of Western civilization. National Socialism was bent on "negating, over
and above liberalism, Christian civilization as such (the breeding-ground
of Modernity and Progress), as well as the Faith which has informed it,
together with some if not most of its sub-soil in Greco-Roman antiquity;
and groping back, in its quest for 'rejuvenating' anti-modern traditions,
across the Prussian glory of yesterday and the more brutal aspects of the
German Middle Ages towards the barbarous world of Teutonic heathen-
dom—not without a side-glance, in my opinion at any rate, at Hindu ra-
cialism and caste religion."[15]

This is what distinguishes Nazism from Fascism. Both are subversive, but for Kolnai, what is essential is whether either offers any shelter
to the abiding values of civilization. He believed no compromise with
Nazism was possible because Nazism saw nothing of value in the institutional sediment of the Enlightenment, of the Christian Middle Ages, or
of Europe's Greco-Roman heritage. Detaching itself from establishment,
it desired a great leap back into the obscure bonds and practices of the
Teutonic tribes. Universal principles of law, of morals, of science, and of
the unity of the human species were all discarded. To the Nazi, Mussolini's Fascistic formula—"*liberty of the state* and of man *in* the state"—was
nowhere near revolutionary enough. It still clung to the idea of distin-
guishable poles: persons and state. But Nazism expressed a "weird idealism of tyranny": the complete abolition of the autonomy of persons in

the will of the state (a flipping from vitalism to angelism). And the state was no mere Roman bureaucracy managing otherwise self-directed lives but was the very vitality of a race sprouting unreservedly in the gestures, voice, and mien of the führer (the impeccable angel). Fascism still thinks in terms of distinction (*WAW,* 580), while Nazism thinks resolutely in terms of identity.

However mangled, ordinary civilizational values find a degree of shelter in the narrowed spaces still left to persons in Fascist politics. Having moved race to the absolute center of its politics, however, Nazism condemned persons to biocentrism and ridded them of will, thought, autonomy, and eccentricity. In consequence, the delicate spanning of personal appetite and civilizational offerings was eliminated in Nazi Germany.

Spengler speaks of "one circle, one type" (*WAW,* 48), Schmitt of the manring, and Stapel of "our moral kinsmen" (*WAW,* 53) and "our national biology" (*WAW,* 288). Summarizing the early twentieth-century cultural historian Arthur Moeller van den Bruck, Kolnai says that tribal egotism (*WAW,* 56) is "the new rebellion in the cause of bondage" (*WAW,* 115)—an "emancipation of tyranny" (*WAW,* 121), wherein "the primary principles of civilized human existence appear reversed" (*WAW,* 121). Thus Nazi literature speaks of a circle of the elect or primaries: a corps or secret society of young unmarried men exhibiting a "swiftly reacting vitality" (*WAW,* 75, 293), who are recipients of the führer's "love-spell" (*WAW,* 77). This circle of vitalism gave rise to a peculiar breed of men, who were a law unto themselves (*WAW,* 36)—a self-idolization (*PVNS,* 49)—and were entrusted with a privileged and revealed knowledge (*WAW,* 60). By contrast, the secondaries were mere breeders and workers. Nazi thinking rejected Burke's "family settlement," preferring the league or sect to the family as a motif (*WAW,* 75): hence, not inheritance, but the stress on "we, the lords of the ultimate decision" (Friedrich Hielscher) (*WAW,* 91).

Kolnai points out that Nazis had a spectrum of religious beliefs. Just as there were some Leftist Nazis, who thought Hitler's labor policies were attractive (*PVNS,* 87), so too were there some Christians, who thought Nazism an actual Christian revival. Kolnai does refer to National Socialism as a Christian heresy, but he spends most of his time documenting the outright paganism of Nazis like Heinrich Himmler and Alfred

Rosenberg. Recognizing that vitalism is at the core of National Social-ism, Kolnai identifies at least three peculiarities separating it from Chris-tianity. All stem from the font of youthful male vitalism.

For Kolnai, Konrad Larenz sets the tone: "All spirit not blood-bound is but a sterile product of decay. Blood must dare to rouse the spirit; spirit must renew itself from blood" (*WAW,* 194). Nazi racism meant that par-ticularism suspended rule of law (*WAW,* 272), generating a "rupture of species" (Rolf Zimmermann) that rejected, in principle, a common mo-rality and destiny for human beings (*WAW,* 279). Its race nationalism meant a rejection of the West's ethos. This reconfirmed its anti-Semitism, just as Athens and Rome are incomplete without Jerusalem (*WAW,* 233–34). Nazis claimed that government earns its legitimacy when it expresses tribal vitalism: only one model of government can reflect this monism, totalitarianism (*PVNS,* 45). Kolnai argues that National Social-ism was an exaggeration of Luther's already-exaggerated valorization of national secular authority: this seam in German theology (*WAW,* 209) gifted the Nazis with a ready obedience to the führer quite out of keeping with Christian skepticism to worldly government. Of course, Nazi anti-Judaism was also amply boosted by its crony capitalism. Jewish cosmo-politanism was said to be responsible for speculative financial markets, but German capitalism aimed at the national social good.

The Bund had a sexuality different from the family. Kolnai points out the significance of homoeroticism in Nazism (*WAW,* 14, 75–76). Hans Blüher is explicit that the family is not the model of the Bund; rather, "man-to-man Eros" is exhibited by those belonging to a genuine anthro-pological species, the *Typus inversus* (*WAW,* 77). "Man is man's relish" (Ernst Bergmann) (*WAW,* 247). This Eros is a "primitive force," an "in-stinct of combination," an "Army metaphysical" (*WAW,* 257), contrast-ing with the sexual impulse that gives rise to births and family (*WAW,* 78): indeed, the life of the Bund is austere and chaste, a veneration of the male body (*WAW,* 82), with an admixture of "Doric harshness" (*WAW,* 78). This biocentrism explains Nazi reprimitivism (*WAW,* 206).

As Kolnai reports, for Blüher, the main forms of human society are rooted in "sexual, erotical, instinctual, irrational forces," but this vital-ism is divided into two principal types: procreative Eros, which issues in the family, and the "inverted love" of man-to-man Eros; together, they are the true origin of state-building (*WAW,* 79). The tribal egotism of the Bund opposes the "banal society" of procreative Eros. The adversary of the Männerbund is "the system of Urbanity" (*WAW,* 89): the femininity of commercial life (*WAW,* 226) and social thinness of business corporations (*WAW,* 80) are opposed to soldiery as the prototype of community (*WAW,* 84). The Nazi is no steward of property, for "nothing is real but ecstasy and ruin, eruption and evanescence" (*WAW,* 209). To the Nazi, "generation, life and murder are one" (Alfred Bäumler, quoted in *WAW,* 592), for "real heroic soldierliness can only subsist as a fundamental law of life in a thoroughly unbourgeois society" (*WAW,* 85, 214). There is no love of the good—whether of persons or the goods of fashion—but only love of the hero (*WAW,* 86): "The Teutons or the Night—is and remains our motto" (Ludwig Schemann, quoted in *WAW,* 582). Kolnai cites Hitler's claim that the struggle for existence annuls "aesthetical obligations" (*WAW,* 173). Thus, according to Rosenberg, "Great history is not made by suave people: it is made by strong men—who are strong because they are *absolutely* hard" (*WAW,* 291).

Pursuing reprimitivism, Bäumler identifies the enemy as the "educated private gentleman of property," who "sets the fashion" (*WAW,* 89–90, 203–4). Hielscher wants to be rid of bourgeois civilization—dismissed as no more than a "cross-conjunction of mere surfaces"—and seeks to replace it with the authenticity of the Bund's brotherhood (*WAW,* 91). Thus Nazism rejects something it rather hilariously identifies as "the English spirit of Viking Liberalism" (*WAW,* 141).

Reprimitivism was offered, contends Kolnai, as "a critical answer to an already existing civilization" (*PVNS,* 45)—the tribe being a willful dismissal and launch into "a dull, unawoken and prejudiced being, lacking the civilized traits of human autonomy, rationality, versatility and world-openness" (*PVNS,* 45). Uniformization (*PVNS,* 51) is consciously opposed to two perceived, complementary agents of universalism: the Catholic Church and humanitarianism (*WAW,* 51–52, 97). Again, in 1938, when he was part of the Christian Left, Kolnai viewed humanitarianism as itself a Christian phenomenon (*WAW,* 103), but by 1944, he had adopted Max Scheler's skepticism toward humanitarianism (see "The Humanitarian versus Religious Attitude" (*PVNS,* 175–96), which is essential Kolnai reading in my opinion). Indeed, by his 1960 essay

"Human Dignity Today" (*PVNS*, 213–16), Kolnai had come to regard humanitarianism's implicit materialism, with its valorization of medical, psychiatric, technological, and economic managerialism, as little more than a repeat of Fascist vitalism.

Reprimitivism is "a backward leap across the ages," "the creation of new things in the spirit of a total inversion of the general trend" (*WAW*, 122). It is, as Kolnai intriguingly says, the shedding of "the garments of civilization" (*PVNS*, 49). Ernst Jünger thrilled to the idea of a Germany of workers all wearing work outfits (*WAW*, 86–87): a Germany exuding contempt for the nonmoral values ordinary life is built around (*WAW*, 139). This is the root of the Nazi rejection of democratic sensibility. A large scope exists for acts of daily living that, even if they do not embellish or perfect human life—reading the sports' pages, say—certainly do not rubbish it, either. The commonly enacted values of ordinary life, most of which are not properly moral, nonetheless create the indispensable condition for flights toward the higher, tone-setting values of a richly articulated, elevated, and moral culture. A proper aristocratic character, rather than that of the specious Nazi variety, must give an egalitarian nod toward a sensibility, in which, for example, politeness can be refined into graciousness (*AE*, 250); the cautious risk-taking of a stolid propertied class can ultimately merge into the extravagance of the fashionable; and common decency can grow into benevolence (a point made in Kolnai's magnificent late essay, "The Concept of Hierarchy"[16]).

In the next chapter, we will test the resilience of this conclusion. Postmodernism is a reaction to the enormity of modernity's failings. It is not a return to the premodern. To acknowledge God is sovereign is no more acceptable than acknowledging the sovereignty of the will (Schopenhauer and Nietzsche), party, and state (Marxism), or a tribe and race (Nazism). Many in the West might shrug their shoulders and think, "well, that's pretty obvious, for we are liberal, fashionable, bourgeois, and humanitarian, so none of those odd, reactionary, and strident things for us." Giorgio Agamben is not convinced. Perhaps the most prominent contemporary European intellectual, Agamben disputes *The War against the West* and poses a deep challenge to my thesis.

Agamben does not accept Kolnai's account of National Socialism as biocentrism but focuses on something Kolnai himself mentions: the vitality of a race sprouting unreservedly from the gestures, voice, and mien of the führer. National Socialism was liturgical and thus in essence was no different from Burke's conservatism (the spirit of the gentleman and religion) or today's liberalism (mild, emotive, and flaunting virtue-signaling brands). The liturgical is not a solution, for Fascism, conservatism and liberalism are just storms in a teacup. They have a unified origin in the church's juridical assertion of liturgy as the way of the church rather than of Franciscan ideals of simplicity.[17] Liturgy has determined the ethics and politics of modernity, and disastrously so.[18] Analyzing National Socialism, Kolnai puts the emphasis on vitalism and Agamben on angelism. The following chapter concerns both the postmodern reaction to modern sovereignty and the start of my defense of natural law. We will want to see whether there is a rigorous way to distinguish among liturgies.

CHAPTER FIVE

AGAMBEN ON THE ONTOLOGY
OF CLOTHES

Modernity was supposed to be the summit of enlightenment and peace, a time when free peoples would exchange ideas and goods to the mutual enhancement of all. No one believes this now, and as early as Burke and Malthus skeptical eyebrows rose. Even before the Communists and Nazis put paid to modernity's rosy self-assessment, Husserl was speaking of a European crisis, in language continued today by Giorgio Agamben. Failure to understand political theology is the reason why contemporary democracy is in crisis, he argues.[1] Adopting Carl Schmitt's insight that each epoch forges a "metaphysical image" legitimizing a particular form of government,[2] Agamben proposes that "long before the terminology of civil administration and government was developed and fixed [in modern states], it was already firmly constituted in angelology."[3] Angels are our image.

The modern history of the West, Schmitt argues, is the stripping away of all institutions able to decentralize, diffuse, and resist power.[4] On the one side, the state, on the other, micromanaged populations—headless bodies, so to say, related to one another through management metrics. Through this decapitation, the angels of the state bureaucracy manage the headless bodies of the people.

The modern history of the West has been percolating since the Middle Ages. Christian theology posited a God both immutable and providential: a transcendent sovereign God, who nonetheless cares for every hair on every head, as said in the Bible. How is it possible to mediate these two poles of the divine? Angels. Medieval treatises on angelology invented the managerial, administrative state. In the Christian theology of providence (*economia*), managing the domestic life of the household (*oikos*) became the task of the angels and, once secularized, the task of the state (God) administrators (angels) of the modern economy. The household—its income, sexuality, education, health, and welfare—is laid bare before the gaze of the state administrators.[5] The state veils its power precisely in those moments when it offers the most care. Power inoculates itself from judgment as care of the family. Beyond the veil, the reality is that each and every family member is exposed to the total and lethal power of the monitoring managerial state.

The crisis of the modern West is that angels have usurped popular sovereignty: self-rule and self-regulating community life are no more.[6] To the contrary, D. G. Leahy writes, "In the mind of God the creature exists absolutely. In the mind of the creature God exists absolutely."[7] A summation of Leahy's thinking, these sentences carry his distinctive account of revelation and identity. The only postmodern Catholic work that rivals *AE* is Leahy's *Beyond Sovereignty*. Leahy reverses Agamben, asserting that national sovereignty is problematic because it restricts our angelism, clipping our wings: "the angelic body that for the first time knows nothing of walls or classes."[8]

I want to use the key claim of Przywara—that a proper accounting of the relationship between creature and creator (sovereign) must defer to analogy—to explore sovereignty in Leahy and Agamben. A theory that argues that the sovereign has no continuity with things natural, customary, or human is not analogical but equivocal (Agamben). A theory that argues that the sovereign is in strict continuity with things natural, customary, and human is univocal (Leahy). For Agamben, the sovereign is the modern corrosive state, its law is abnormally formed because it is haughty, out of symmetry with all things natural, customary, and human. He rejects the sovereign (equivocity).[9] For Leahy, God is sovereign but so utter is this sovereignty that customary or national law is suspended in the unity of action, both divine and human. Indeed, so fused are divine and human action that each and every discrete act is sovereign (univocity). Whether beyond sovereignty equivocally or univocally, national or civil law is not really law at all. The Przywarian analogical alternative will emerge below, as I detail further both the dispute between Leahy and Agamben and why they are critical of sovereignty.

What makes *Beyond Sovereignty* so dense is its metaphysical rigor. What type of ethical theory relies so extensively on metaphysics? Natural law. Natural law is not especially popular today, not even in Catholic theology. University textbooks on philosophy of law or moral theory seldom mention it. For the secular academy, it is thought too theistic and too traditional, running counter to progressivism's interest in abortion, gay marriage, and sexual identity. The American Jesuit John Courtney Murray quips that philosophers congratulate themselves on burying natural law, only to discover they have buried the wrong body.[10] Leahy's natural law theory is a case in point: it is so unexpected, so original.

Some theorists defend natural law as an account of rationality, as a set of inferences from rational axioms. I have always been more persuaded by Saint John Paul the Great's treatment of natural law as a metaphysical and value account of the body. The rationalists minimize the embodied inclinations that Thomas appears to make important in his theory. John Paul II takes natural law to be a theory of desire. Leahy does not develop his theory obviously from either reason or desire, but, as with John Paul II, the emphasis is firmly on a metaphysics of the body, with flesh startlingly thought of as a sort of Angelic greeting (*Beyond*, 133).

Like Thomistic natural law, Leahy deploys his version as a political ethics, doing so amid a sustained treatment of Agamben. In spite of his admiration of Agamben, Leahy seeks to correct his account of vanity. This account is somewhat unusual in rather cleverly glossing the emptiness of vanity as free potency, a sort of leisured ableness. Agamben casts vanity as inoperativity, that is, the human released from work, released from commodities, released from the state's micromanagement. Vanity, interrupting action,[11] suspends the state's sovereignty, dedicated as it is to busy management of populations as economic *materiel*. This understanding of vanity is peculiar and, I believe, problematic, but Leahy thinks it mistakes the nature of what sovereignty targets. In Agamben, the body liberated from modern politics is potency no longer forced to act, but for Leahy the body is never reserved (*Beyond*, 209; *Foundation*, 577), for "the body itself, the infinite surface,"(189) is the body offering, foundationally readiness (*Beyond,* 87, 192): "the beginning in reserve, the buried talent, has now been taken away and given" (*Foundation,* 580). Thus at the heart of Leahy's natural law is that "essence *is* the absolutely objective I otherwise than presence" (*Beyond,* 219).

In *Beyond Sovereignty,* Leahy does not, as in Agamben, push the self to a vanishing point, making the self *inapparent* (Agamben's term). For this effectively does the bidding of sovereignty: the point rather is to expose sovereignty's containment as illicit by casting it as a brake on the fertility of action. Being wells up at each and every point, breaking the point in offering. Angels are not at any point in space because they are always offering service that others might flourish. So the body as offering is not at any point, neither in space nor in governmental space, but is always, already, and everywhere—edge (*Foundation,* 591). Action is always beyond itself—assisting, steadying, opening ways, and giving competency. This is higher law, which national or civil law threatens: the body as angelic offering is a rebuke to any sovereignty, any national law (a sort of false self) that would wall (*Beyond,* 223) or clamp down on the action of "upbuilding" (*Foundation,* 578).

Action has its wellspring in the following unity: "In the mind of God the creature exists absolutely. In the mind of the creature God exists absolutely" (*Foundation,* 579). I understand that Leahy is playing on the meaning of "absolutely" (*ab-solutus*/detached), trying to put some distance between creaturely mind and the divine, but still the unity between the two is too forcefully stated (univocity). The proof is clothes and fashion. Vanity is the culminating dispute between Leahy and Agamben, yet both trip up. Agamben overuses vanity, while Leahy rids us of it. Stressing the emptiness of vanity, Agamben seeks to use the metaphysical thinness of vanity against the spectating power of the managerial state (equivocity). In Aquinas, vanity is a barometer of the self, the story a self tells (revelation) about its relations to God and others (identity).[12] Such is the clarifying power of revelation in Leahy that he rids us of vanity metaphysically; the possibility of conceit—conceit of self and establishment/sovereignty—is removed (univocity).

Leahy notes, "Existence itself for the first time the existence of the passion of Christ" (184), but Christ, the passion of Christ, is Christ stripped bare, Christ naked. Thus, when Leahy writes that the person is a selfless offering, surface opened 360 degrees, Christ without Christ, in other words, Christ not enthroned but Christ offering—"the absolute passion of existence" (*Beyond,* 185)—and "for the first time the very essence of identity" (*Beyond,* 184), I say, here there is a problem, that *I* am not naked. I know this is to challenge Leahy's most central contention: beyond modernity there is no self; flesh, so often thought selfish, manipulating, vain, is constitutively global, flesh everywhere offering (*Beyond,* 39). However, it is my contention that Leahy, following a drive in twentieth-century philosophy to ever seek out the more elemental ground of thought and being, has in fact detached his thinking from a stubborn and recalcitrant phenomenon, but not for these reasons one that is immoral: ornamentation.[13] We decorate ourselves with clothes, and though clothes do realize Leahy's *unum*/with, they do not as "out absolutely with/with itself out" (*Beyond,* 185). Clothes are an index of civilization, and with them we form a conceit (Shaftesbury), a story, for ourselves, and about ourselves for others (vanity). In this story, veneration (God), refinement (establishment), and style (self) are *plaited together* (Przywara). Ornamentation is a sway in the metaphysical order that blocks both equivocity and univocity.

Following Przywara, sovereignty is akin to a suspension bridge: it links, because it defers to, two discrete but related standings, God and the self. Sovereignty suspended between the two is establishment, and human life finds its fullness when *plaited* (*AE,* 265) together with God (veneration) and establishment (refinement). This is sovereignty analogically understood: establishment is not God but reveals him (not univocal), and conceit is not possible without establishment,[14] yet the self must still stylize (not equivocal).

Leahy writes, "Without plan or plane for the first time conceived in essence Omnipotence itself is indeed absolute nimbleness" (*Beyond,* 209). I say, the human body has height and disguise by ornament; ornament is the conceit of self, and this is as structural a feature of human life as any other phenomenon needing moral and political analysis. Evidence suggested by genetic changes in lice dates clothing to around 170,000 years ago, about the same time as the oldest human remains.[15] David Hume thought humans constitutively ornamental. Leahy does not disagree, but his response is nuanced: "What now for the first time is conceived essentially is the Apocalyptic vision: there is no temple in the city, nothing whatsoever is hidden, the body itself is clothing itself, clothes do not cover the body but reveal the essence of the body, manifest the essentially artifactual structure of the body, reveal the world to be such a novelty that man cannot stand even so much apart as to be a participant, so as to (merely) *take* part in the creation of the world, avoiding thereby the absolute responsibility of creating a new world" (*Foundation*, 592).

Agamben hollows out the self, whereas Leahy turns the self inside out. Clothes, however, show the self skips away. Leahy agrees with Hume that the human is constitutively artifactual, but what are clothes? As Agamben pushes you and me to the inapparent, so Leahy makes us all too apparent. Body as *unum*/with: "The God of Revelation has absolutely no secrets. Omnipotence itself absolutely exposed—absolutely outside—for the first time" (*Beyond*, 208). The decorated body is not this exorbitant, for clothes as ornament are also style, panache, and flair, and this is what the West's philosophical tradition tries to capture in talk of the self. Style is a witness both to establishment from which it draws and to the self. Decorated clothing plaits together establishment and self. *And this is to also say* that there is a place for customary and national law, a place for sovereignty. Decoration gives my body geography, an embossing,[16] and sovereignty is similarly ornamental, a knot of law and land, a plaited commons, the abiding of establishment, family, and self.

Beyond Sovereignty closes with a discussion of Agamben's analysis of Titian's *Nymph and Shepherd* (c. 1576). In this picture of two lovers resting after sex, the nymph is mostly naked and seen from behind, while the shepherd is clothed. About the Titian, Agamben glosses, "Beyond concealment and disconcealment these lovers have initiated each other into their own lack of mystery as their most intimate secret; they mutually forgive each other and expose their *vanitas*. Bare or clothed, they are no longer either concealed or unconcealed—but rather, inapparent" (*Beyond*, 220). They are no longer object for a subject; intentionality is suspended, still in consciousness but now consciousness not working but "perfectly inoperative." The inapparent is workless, without identity, and Leahy glosses that "their 'most intimate secret' is their emptiness, their *vanitas*—out in the open" (*Beyond*, 221). Cleverly, Agamben uses vanity against itself. Its emptiness is used to empty sovereignty of its grip on us, a grip fostered by fashion and spectacle.

Agamben believes himself to have found a new field of study, the "choreography of power" (*KG,* 184): the science of "acclamations, ceremonies, liturgies, and insignia" (*KG,* 188). He argues that the imagistic character of contemporary politics is akin to the liturgy of the Catholic Mass. In each, power (kingdom) dresses and masks itself (government) (*KG,* 168, 256). Whether it is the mass or fashion design, we are all now in thrall, declares Agamben, to "the society of the spectacle" (*KG,* xii). Imagistic politics preoccupies us, seductively wrapping government, while kingdom hides: we no more practice political self-rule than did medieval serfs.

Adam Smith's observations about the spectator and celebrity fashion (*KG,* 255–56), provides Agamben evidence:[17] "Liturgy and *oikonomia* are, from this perspective, strictly linked, since as much in the songs and the acclamations of praise as in the acts of the priest, it is always only 'the economy of the Savior'"(*KG,* 173, 188). Agamben is fond of a Byzantine ritual manual that speaks of the need to project royal power into a mirror: central to power is the image (*KG,* 184). Fascism was masterful at liturgical politics, but progressivism is not shoddy either. Imagistic politics, with the cooperation of design, fashion, celebrity, songs, and pop videos, seeks out "consecrated symbols" (*KG,* 188). Left and Right have a fondness for "messiahs." Agamben worries that the rule of salvific government (angelic gaze) trades on the "inseparable brothers" (*KG,* 285) veneration and refinement. It is the discontinuity between the reality and appearance of authority that gives power its obscure, lurking, menacing quality.

Agamben published these particular arguments after 2010 and the publication of *Beyond Sovereignty.* However, they are only color for firmly stated arguments in prior Agamben books that were addressed by Leahy. In *Ecstatic Morality,* I show that John Paul II's theology of the body relies on a high Christology—Christ, an offering metaphysical, the very order of natural law. Leahy's theology is also a Christological metaphysics: "the beginning of the body, of society, of the new humanity conceived essentially, i.e., conceived qua historical actuality as *the Artifactual body of Jesus Christ*" (*Foundation,* 578; italics in original). For this reason, Leahy is committed to an equally high account of R/revelation. In an important passage, he writes, "The new necessity is the absolutely 'artifactual' body. The absolute context *is* an absolutely unconditioned individuality.

The absolutely self-less apocalypse, the revelation/revolution beginning" (*Foundation*, 560).

Does clothing support Leahy? Does clothing allow any such revelation of unconditioned individuality? No matter my style, my cunning, or my original articulation of what I have received, I rely on establishment. What I dispute is the metaphysical opportunity for "the incipient existence of the absolute upbuilding of infinite totalities" (*Foundation*, 578). Being human, being moral—natural law—is not so liquid as Leahy wants it to be.

I am not an infinite totality because I am decorated, and this is especially true in an age of fashion. I inherit and defer to the patterns (value tones), labor, logistics, and capital of others. Decoration is a deferential or obediential attitude to establishment, a bow to the sovereignty of objects. Leahy writes, "In the mind of God the creature exists absolutely. In the mind of the creature God exists absolutely. This is for the first time the *absolute* analogy of being. . . . *The Name* identically *for the first time* the embodied soul's consciousness of its *essentially corporeal*, i.e., *artifactual, relation to God*, for the first time its awareness of its Body-of-Christ-essence, at once its incipient knowledge, in the form of the absolute readability of identity and the body, of every other existent" (*Foundation*, 579; italics in original).

I think Leahy is right that there is a "readability of identity and the body," for establishment conveys value tones. In other words, sovereignty is deferential, too: bound by an order of values that it tracks and embodies. Agamben and Leahy both overstate the problem of sovereignty, therefore. To obey establishment is actually to bow to a value hierarchy expressed through establishment. Fashion sometimes expresses this directly when, for example, we dress for public occasions (when attending weddings and operas, when appearing before law courts and when courting someone, and even when going to football matches), but it always expresses the value hierarchy no matter the occasion. Think only of design, whether you are contemplating gardens, iPhones, cars, or houses.

Przywara replaces Agamben's angelic management and Leahy's angelic exuberance with a habited humanism in a venerating, bowing posture. Our fashionable conceits exhibit a comparable "posture of distance" to establishment and God (*AE,* 197, 375).

Leahy's ethics is a maximalist metaphysics, and to such a degree that the body as exterior is as Christ exposed, that is, love is at the core of reality unreservedly exposed, naked. Thus, it is hard to know what could ever be the other side of this natural law, or what, if anything, about the human could clip the flight of the human. The moral tradition has focused on moral failure, and then typically wanted to account for that as a matter of inner propensities—Mandeville's vile tubes—the innards of the body,[18] but Leahy's physical ethics relies on the body as pure surface, the body always exposed, the body innocent, the body not making a show of itself but showing itself in offering—namely, as sacrifice without remainder. Clothing suggests, however, that the moral tradition has a careful eye.

Leahy's global ethics runs counter to Mandeville's egoist ethics, and one reason, among many, that Leahy is so interesting is because he rightly presses the egoist on the assumption of a self as an ego isolated from other such detached ego persons. Clearly, Augustine's *Confessions* gives a solid philosophical date for a vivid account of the self, but as late as Aquinas's argument with Averroes—whether there is a universal mind to which human bodies attach or whether there are discrete conscious selves—the Augustinian belief in the self was hardly settled. Leahy is quick to point out that in Aristotle, the soul is a community soul: its character as a form manifests as a fecund act for propagation and social standing (*Beyond*, 196); in like manner, Darwinian ethics also thinks of the "self" as a commons, as a communal history and fund of fertility. Even Aquinas did not think of the human soul as an originally unique particular but as a species made into a discrete singular through union with matter and thus set in space and time.[19]

However murky the intellectual origins of the self, the fact of clothing and adornment suggests that Adam Smith's declaration that people make parade of their riches and conceal their poverty is a profound insight.[20] It is one shared by Aquinas. Leahy sets his face firmly against this. The infinite surface is "absolutely exposed—absolutely outside" (*Beyond*, 208). *Beyond Sovereignty* is the body/Christ always already ecstatic. Decoration is moral, even though this ruptures Leahy's account of persons as metaphysical donation. I appreciate that for Leahy I imply that clothes are vehicles for "the absolute avoidance of responsibility, in the form of the self forgiving forgiving itself self" (*Foundation*, 577), but I hope I have shown that vanity is a "posture of distance" to self and other. This gap is sufficient to sustain morals and civilization. Lacan is also committed to a similarly productive opening, albeit with a different emphasis.

Agamben wants to press the claim that liturgy is the source of re-primitivism, but Przywara shows that a confused metaphysics of morals, rather than establishment (liturgical sovereignty), is responsible. Agamben's own use of vanity, separating itself from the "garments of civilization" (Kolnai), puts a definite emphasis on vitalism and prompts a decapitation. To my mind, Agamben is influenced by Bakunin's biocentrism[21] and runs the risk of backing into the vitalism Kolnai identifies in *The War against the West*.

As mentioned in chapter 2, Agamben looks to Peter John Olivi, and monks generally, for inspiration. Hostile to the managerial state, Agamben is interested in nonjuridical communities, of which monasteries at their inception are an example. We saw in chapter 2 that Olivi is an unreliable friend to any anarchist, but Agamben's reading of Olivi confirms the equivocal character of his thinking. Agamben offers Olivi as a medieval reformer of modernity (!) because he is the first to clearly see the ontology of law and management that props up the modern sovereign power.[22] His insight was occluded by the church's deployment and intensification of liturgy. Seeking to open a space outside of law,[23] Olivi affirmed the absolute disjunction of law (essence) and way of life (existence). He sought "a pure and absolutely inessential command" that would contest law and liturgy: "form of life is the purely existential reality that must be liberated from the signature of law and office or duty."[24]

Agamben is certainly right that not all liturgy is good liturgy, but his unrestrained equivocity pushes him to vitalism and a decapitation in metaphysics. I will have to offer ways to distinguish among liturgies (games and value tones), but, as Przywara ably shows, it is *analogia entis* that avoids totalitarianism and offers the metaphysics of morals that can support a rule of law. Let us now look at how Merleau-Ponty builds a "posture of distance" into the body.

CLOTHES AND MERLEAU-PONTY'S FLESH

The Visible and the Invisible is a brilliant reflection on the body. Although studies of the body have mushroomed since its publication in 1964, Merleau-Ponty's role is unclear.[1] Despite its brilliance, the book suggests that Merleau-Ponty missed something absolutely crucial about our embodiment: biopolitics. *Biopolitics* is Foucault's term for his insight that the body is the point of application of sovereign power. This insight has proved electric. With Agamben, biopolitics becomes the claim that investigation of the body requires political theology, and he seems persuaded by Bakunin's options: either bureaucracy (angelism) or nature (vitalism).[2]

Why return to Merleau-Ponty, whose phenomenology inquires into the body apart from establishment and its techniques of punishment, labor, medicine, war, and sex? He helps my argument move forward because his flesh is clothed. It is noteworthy that his phenomenology of the body relies heavily on motifs of textiles, tailoring, and style (*VI*, 115).[3] About the color red, he writes "It is a certain node in the woof of the simultaneous and the successive. It is a concretion of visibility, it is not an atom. The red dress a fortiori holds with all its fibers onto the fabric of the visible, and thereby onto a fabric of invisible being" (*VI*, 132).

Przywara's central claim is that the creature is a "posture of distance." In the next three chapters, I will show that this is a potent formulation of the meaning of natural law, which explains why flesh is always the rule of law (as we saw with Thomas Reid in chapter 3). This first of the three chapters discusses Merleau-Ponty's description of flesh as "lace-works," which he offers as a criticism of Max Scheler's hierarchy of values (*VI*, 270). Yet his phenomenological description of flesh as "lace-works" complicates matters for him. His three preferred motifs—biology, dress, and landscape—all point to the body as ornamental and articulated in ludic gesture. What Merleau-Ponty calls "this Baroque world."[4]

This moves my argument forward: Przywara's posture (vitalism) of distance (angelism) breaks up the diplopia of Bakunin. *Diplopia,* a term Merleau-Ponty borrows from the Catholic philosopher Maurice Blondel,[5] gives *The Visible and the Invisible* structural concerns very like those in *Analogia Entis*. Bakunin and Agamben seek to free the body of state sovereignty. They are right to want to be rid of managerial law. Merleau-Ponty shows that interior to flesh is decoration, marriage, family, and play—in short, liturgy. The body is already the rule of law, and managerial law is excessive law. Law is part of play, however, and ritual does not happen outside of establishment: state sovereignty is compatible with natural law. Modernity's humanism is failing because state sovereignty is either excessive (univocity) or remiss (equivocity), and more often than not both. Merleau-Ponty's flesh avoids decapitation by affirming naturalism and establishment.

Merleau-Ponty is Pope Gregory VII's heir, in that his phenomenology of flesh shows how a metaphysics of morals helps adjudicate ethical problems. In particular, his account of flesh as clothed helps us think through moral questions raised by clothes. Is a sumptuary law excessive managerial law? One of the most delicate moral questions in the West today is how to respond to the desire of Muslims for Sharia law or, at the very least, their desire for public recognition of modesty in the West. A related problem is how Western business ought to respond to the rising demand for "modest wear." Leahy and Agamben are so insightful because their argument over sovereignty comes back to an argument about vanity. In the last few decades, life in the West has been radically altered by war and terrorism and an upswing in administrative law to manage the consequences (this fact is the goad for Agamben's work). Starting in the late 1960's, legal rulings about abortion provoked the resurgence of political Catholicism, typified by the intellectual papacies of Saint John Paul II and Benedict XVI.

Political Islam is a more recent phenomenon in the West, and its focus can be fairly summed up, I think, as a dispute about vanity. We ought not to be surprised: Plato's *Republic* is about the same issue. Indeed, a close look at our greatest theoreticians shows that almost all think about vanity and ornament. Merleau-Ponty, with his dressed flesh, is a case in point, as is Edmund Burke, whom we see more of in this chapter.

The Visible and the Invisible is a careful phenomenology that reveals decapitation (diplopia) as a false accounting of the ontic and noetic. Flesh (ontic) is not speech (noetic)—there is a distance—but there is also a "prolongation" of being in speech (*VI*, 118). Merleau-Ponty argues against idealism in Husserl and materialism in Sartre. Indeed, in a very Przywarian way, he notes in particular of Sartre that his thinking flips back and forth between angelism and vitalism. Merleau-Ponty is in some ways similar to Schopenhauer in his formulation that the visible (object) and invisible (idea and sonorous vortex or undertow of the visible) are flesh doubling (*VI*, 114): this double aspect means that both theopanism (idealism) and pantheism (vitalism) are bad accountings of reality. He is after something like the *analogia entis*, therefore, and the doubling that puts a distance between object and idea edges toward Reid's gestural body (natural language).

The relationship between object and idea is interior to flesh, a furrow (*VI*, 151), a splitting open (dehiscence).[6] In this way, Merleau-Ponty avoids univocity and equivocity because object and experience are co-originals: as in Przywara, the model is a suspension of ontic (being) and noetic (speech) (*AE*, 124). At one point, Merleau-Ponty says he is not doing anthropology, but Reid's gestural body presses the question: Can we separate flesh from ritual? We will see that Merleau-Ponty concedes the point.

His preferred motifs of biology, dress, and landscape help Merleau-Ponty avoid angelism (the Cartesian tradition culminating in Husserl's idealist essentialism), but he does not want to back into vitalism (a shredded plurality of drives). When beautifully casting flesh as "open vortexes in the sonorous world" (*VI*, 151), Merleau-Ponty edges into the phenomenon of play. His effort to steer clear of angelism and vitalism means flesh intimates that body (existence) is internally a value tone (essence) lived playfully (*AE*, 126–28) and ritually, and thus as law.[7]

In a 1960 working note to *The Visible and the Invisible,* Merleau-Ponty describes flesh as "lace-works." Drawn from fashion and craft, the image conveys that being is a visible and invisible expanse (as lace is presence and absence). The visible—our experience of the myriad objects of the world—is a series of differentiations in "massive flesh." This visibility has an obverse, invisibility, that itself has a double meaning. On the one hand, the invisible is a collective name for our ideas or conceptualizations—these object-contents are not visible in the way objects are—and on the other, the invisible is a collective name for a "raw being," a real undertow, or "occult" (*VI,* 183), that births the visible and our conceptualizations.

How to think about the invisible is the nub of Merleau-Ponty's dispute with Scheler (*VI,* 270). Can one think of this undertow without conceding Scheler's theory of values? Merleau-Ponty admits that "the most difficult point" addressed in *The Visible and the Invisible* is the bond between flesh and idea, between the visible and "the interior armature" or "whole architecture" of flesh that the visible manifests and conceals (*VI,* 149, 114). Certain ideas in our minds map this armature because a prolongation of it (*VI,* 151). These ideas span the ontic and noetic, world and mind; indeed, both world and mind open up inside these ideas (*VI,* 152). Music, literature, and the passions, but not the sciences, convey these ideas. The arts and reason, rather than science, give us the surest truth, the reason being that science is all too well aware of the visible and cannot appreciate that the visible manifests *and* conceals. Science is an investigation into causality and aims for a complete description of objects that implicitly relies on the mentalism of Cartesian metaphysics (*VI,* 206). Just as the "backside" of the rose bush outside my window is hidden from me, and just as objects take on specificity as the mind isolates them from rapid perceptual changes and their identity-in-an-expanse, so too does scientific exactitude, in pressing visibility, conceal (*VI,* 136). It is an abstraction of objects that grants far too great a scope to mental definitional operations (*VI,* 213; Descartes's res cogitans is too much a noetics). Merleau-Ponty's baroque world teems with "ultra things."[8]

Merleau-Ponty's doubling is an effort to block the temptation to Cartesian (and Parmenidian) univocity. It has continuities with Schopenhauer's double-aspect theory and Przywara's suspension, but what is most remarkable is the degree to which Merleau-Ponty accords coherence to the invisible. He must be delicate. He means to escape the noetics of res cogitans, with its heavy emphasis on the subject (angelism), but he does not want to back into naïve realism, in which the subject has no role, and collapse into materialism (vitalism). He casts the invisible as "vaginal" potency (*VI*, 115, 124, 209) of "the wild region" (*VI*, 115)—what Przywara in his phenomenology of civilizations describes as Etruscan (*AE*, 489–90), or what Shaftesbury, Reid, and Scheler describe as value tones.

Merleau-Ponty is fond of landscape as a motif to capture the differentiations internal to flesh. Shaftesbury offers a gloriously fine-grained phenomenology of landscape:

> Behold the disposition and order of these finer sorts of apartments, gardens, and villa! The kind of harmony to the eye from the various shapes and colours agreeably mixed and ranged in lines, intercrossing without confusion and fortunately coincident. A parterre, cypresses, groves, wildernesses. Statues, here and there, of virtue, fortitude, temperance. Heroes' busts, philosophers' heads, with suitable mottoes and inscriptions. Solemn representations of things deeply natural. Caves, grottoes, rocks. Urns and obelisks in retired places and disposed at proper distances and points of sight, with all those symmetries which silently express a reigning order, peace, harmony and beauty.[9]

This description—and I assume all find it convincing—is replete with value tones and hierarchy. One could imagine a garden built around the ghoulish, but there would be something pointed and self-conscious about it. A garden featuring the virtues—heroic, intellectual, and religious—is not only not absurd but "deeply natural."

Drawing on Proust's account of music, Merleau-Ponty appears to concede the point: "The performer is no longer producing or reproducing the sonata: he feels himself, and the others feel him to be at the service of the sonata; the sonata sings through him or cries out so suddenly that he must 'dash on his bow' to follow it" (*VI*, 151). A quotation from Proust's *Swann's Way* follows immediately: "Never was the spoken language so inflexibly necessitated, never did it know to such an extent the pertinence of the questions, the evidence of the responses" (*VI*, 151).

Not only does Merleau-Ponty give voice to value tones, but the subject (speech) is cast as gesture, play, and obedience. The musician obeys the sonata; he is in the grip of a vortex of the sonorous world. Przywara would say the same (*AE*, xxii, and especially 158–59n6). This vortex in being speaks as a gesture, the dashing of the bow, and the spectators in black tie will the player on, desperate for their sensibilities and his to be aligned with "a reigning order." "The pregnancy is what, in the visible, requires of me a *correct* focusing, defines its correctness. My body *obeys* the pregnancy, it 'responds' to it, it is what is suspended on it, flesh responding to flesh" (*VI*, 209; italics in original). Though Merleau-Ponty does not draw out the point, here we see a hint of biopolitics: for opera; ballet; and chamber, symphonic, and church music are all part of establishment. Our sensibility is flooded with the visible (objects of awareness), the fecund discretion of a "carnal texture" "that traces itself out magically under our eyes without a tracer." The ideas are from neither the world nor the mind but span the two—"the original ecstasy"[10]—a fertility opening making each possible; Merleau-Ponty calls this gravid suspension flesh and Przywara refers to it as *potentia obedientialis*.

In Merleau-Ponty's phenomenology, the musician obeys the sonata. Aurel Kolnai, another phenomenologist, observes a bow to the sovereignty of objects. Edmund Burke adds that this bow is always a bow to establishment, the settled institutions of a people: for example, the civil service, diplomatic corps, the military and its famous regiments, the courts, universities, churches, the pub, the football pitch, and the cricket green. Each of these institutions house and express value clusters, and, profoundly, deference to these is also a refusal to use power to manipulate objects contrary to their natures.[11] Indeed, for Merleau-Ponty (though not for Shaftesbury), we *suffer* "intentional threads around certain knots," which are "upright, insistent, flaying our glance with their edges."[12]

Value theorists defend a realist account of values claiming that humans have ready access to discrete, extramental value tones: for example, if I say "peach," the taste and smell of a peach, not a lemon, will come to mind. We can replicate this value tone with lip balm, soda, and even gin, once we have distilled it into a chemical formula. Morals have a similar value standing: if I tell you a story about how I met a benefactor, or about a civil chat I had with a man on a train, whose conversation suddenly flashed with malice, your mind will leap to a range of value tones that make these encounters comprehensible.

This theory can trace its heritage to Plato and Aquinas, but the Earl of Shaftesbury speaks for them all, writing, "There is a power in numbers, harmony, proportion and beauty of every kind, which naturally captivates the heart and raises the imagination to an opinion or conceit of something majestic and divine."[13] These thinkers believe that civilizations exist to ensure the refinement of human persons and refinement requires deference to the range of moral, aesthetic, and technical values acknowledged to stand above us.[14] Burke is perhaps the most eloquent proponent of the theory, and, as I have shown, Merleau-Ponty concedes the point in his account of flesh as lace-works.

A contemporary of Merleau-Ponty (d. 1961), Albert Camus (d. 1960) often spoke of his love of swimming in the Mediterranean Sea. As Camus was hyperaware of France's complicated relationship with the Arab world, it would be fascinating to know how he would have reacted to the recent burkini ban on the French Riviera. What of Merleau-Ponty? Can we draw a link between the "close-woven fabric of the true world" (*VI*, 6) and France's new sumptuary law?

The burkini is an example of "modest wear." To many Muslims, the bikini is immodest. Can a metaphysics of morals help adjudicate the controversy? If we grant that Merleau-Ponty provides a careful phenomenology of the body, then flesh seems immodest. Here are a few examples of his descriptions: flesh is "a perpetual pregnancy," "a common nervure," which "by a promiscuity" piles up objects of experience encroaching on one another: this occurs "because a sort of dehiscence opens my body in two" (*VI*, 115, 118, 123), causing it to "be spread out on display" (*VI*, 119).

This language in a philosophical treatise in the 1960s must have made for startling reading, but now the matter is a serious moral dispute with real consequences for the functioning of French society. I do not want to focus on the jarring images of police ham-fistedly trying to impose the ban literally on the beaches, or on the patently false claim from the Muslim head of the UN Commission on Human Rights that the burkini has nothing to do with matters of "public order." No one can accept that clothes and how you style yourself have no meaning or are matters of cultural indifference.

The beach scenes coming from France are examples of biopolitics. I want to assess the justice of the sumptuary law and whether Marks and Spencer is right to sell the burkini.[15] Stated more broadly, is there such a thing as a national brand, and, in consequence, is such a business morally obliged to support its particular civilization? Believing the answer to be "yes," the Socialist government of France has criticized Marks and Spencer. My contention in this book is that a metaphysics of morals can help with our contemporary moral problems. Thus, to inquire whether gravid flesh is immodest is to inquire into the moral standing of the burkini and a business plan that makes it possible.

"In her view what she wears is her own business—and no one else's, a right she thinks that should be enjoyed by all women everywhere." This quote ends a recent *New York Times* article on the burkini and expresses the view of a Muslim woman who wants to wear one.[16] Putting religion to the side, let's assess the truth of this statement. It is clearly false. Were I to walk into a new class wearing a Star Trek bodysuit and in all seriousness start to teach, that would be an issue. I'd look awful, but even if I did look like Jim Kirk, it would still be an issue. Students would rightly think I was not serious-minded and likely would feel that I was even imposing on their generosity far too much. Quite apart from food and safety regulations, the costumes for the games we play, the professions that require dress up, and modesty laws, there is a large array of social norms requiring dress compliance: funerals, black-tie occasions, girls' night out, First Communion, meeting the in-laws for the first time, and so on. There is a hideous song by Miley Cyrus, "We Can't Stop," containing the line "it's my mouth I'll say what I want to."[17] Again, this is simply false. It is equally false whether you are on university grounds or at the local car parts shop.

What about business? Does "we'll sell what we want to" ring any more true? Marks and Spencer's has recently been criticized by the women's rights minister of the ruling French Socialist government for investing in the "Islamic garment market." Pierre Bergé, long-time partner of legend Yves Saint Laurent, has this to say: "Creators should have nothing to do with Islamic fashion. Designers are there to make women more beautiful, to give them their freedom, not to collaborate with this dictatorship which imposes this abominable thing by which we hide women

and make them live a hidden life."[18] Bergé is the very definition of establishment, and his dense statement references a number of values and
disvalues. A full unpacking of these values would take some time, but
Western fashion defers to beauty, liberty, visibility, and mobility. Let's
take this paraphrase of a passage from Bergé's statement: the burkini is no
part of the trajectory of Western fashion. As a piece of clothing, there is
nothing playful about the burkini. It is not ornamental, nor does it have
panache. Designed to obscure flesh, it is a decapitation. It is the vitalism
of skin occluded by angelism: the body taken up unreservedly into divine
law (univocity). Bergé thinks the burkini and dictatorship go hand-in-
hand, and, as we saw in the introduction, Przywara shows how decapitation serves tyranny.

Let's take it as uncontroversial that there are national brands: James
Bond, Aston Martin, Burberry, Mulberry, Ferrari, Hermès, Cucinelli,
and, among many others, that staple of the British high street, M&S. Is a
national brand obliged to affirm the values sustaining its own civilization?

Among political factions, libertarians and conservatives likely struggle
most with this question. The liberal humanitarian will surely think M&S
must sell the burkini as part of its corporate social responsibility obligation to globalism, and specifically British multiculturalism. For the liberal
humanitarian, national obligations make no sense.

Libertarians are allergic to corporate social responsibility. They deny
that social justice obligations are implied by property holding, preferring the claim that holding property in business is for the sake of making money, and it is entirely up to the discretion of property owners how
they spend that money. However, many libertarians also recognize that
this view of property is a legacy of long philosophical and legal medita-
tion, and they get nervous when a staple of the British high street like
M&S departs so significantly from Western fashion. Libertarians are not
insensitive to the idea that a culture broadly committed to riches, vanity,
fashion, and autonomy helps sustain a robust account of property rights.

Conservatives, meanwhile, are faced with a very sticky wicket. They
don't much care for corporate social responsibility as it is typically expressed, but they do have their own variants, linked perhaps to virtue
theory (MacIntyre), distributism (Scheler), or Catholic Social Thought.
In contrast to libertarians, therefore, they do strongly believe that businesses

have all manner of ethical obligations. Unlike the humanitarian liberal, however, they think M&S has an obligation to support those values that have long sustained the company. Moreover, the appeal of the burkini to the value of modesty will not be lost on the conservative. The puzzle is whether a modesty claim quite outside the trajectory of Western fashion is acceptable. We must also examine whether the bikini is immodest.

Burke argues that the institutional life of a nation must follow the "method of nature" if it is to be happy and successful. Burke did not think that the arc of history bends toward justice but instead worried about the fragility of civilization. He preferred thinking of the polity as "the original plant."[19] This gardening motif makes politics a careful cultivation of an inheritance. While still retaining their identity, plants change to suit the season and so must politics: stewardship is not the same as embalming rigidity, but it also does not experiment with fundamental, sweeping change, for this would be to treat "the original plant" as no better than a weed. Politics must operate with deference to the contours of the plants and how they shape the garden (the theological warrant for this idea can be found in Dante's Eternal Gardener).

Politics functions in "the spirit of philosophic analogy," and along the lines of the garden motif is politics as "family settlement." Institutions change—they have a history—but they also have stable coordinates in space and time. Similar to a family, an institution will have a past (history), present (place), and future (trajectory). In the natural world, creatures thrive by balancing inheritance, territory, and reproduction. Families and institutions are the same. Note that Burke uses analogy in the sense Przywara does: politics is suspended across past, present, and future. Note, too, how this meets Merleau-Ponty's goal of embodiment as neither univocal nor equivocal but as the "natal pact" of world and mind.[20] A political act modeled on flesh is never an adequation to itself, for it is always deference to an inheritance it did not make and is in service to a future it cannot manage.

The very idea of a brand, especially a national brand, expresses an inheritance. In "business speak," that is a company's DNA, and sometimes it is coincident quite literally with family DNA (this is true of Ford, Toyota, Fendi, and Cucinelli, to name just a few businesses with abiding family connections). This inheritance is also a place: a brand has a geography. Companies need to think about logistics, risk, environment, materials, personnel, capital, and design precisely because they have geographical identities. For these reasons, M&S is Western, and, as Pierre Bergé points out, to be Western means to defer to a particular cluster of values—aesthetic, political, moral, and technical—that are the inner bearings of a brand's trajectory.

Brands have become unstuck before, precisely by losing sight of their value geography. The burkini is a decapitation, and unsurprisingly M&S's desire to profit from the "modest wear" market is a decapitation. An appetite for profit without deference to establishment is no longer a posture of distance. The burkini is divine law without reserve (idea and univocity), and M&S is unrestrained appetite for profit (vitalism and equivocity). The burkini is a modesty claim but not a moral one.

Perhaps it is not a moral claim because a bikini is not, in fact, immodest? Is flesh itself immodest? The bikini meets the definition of laceworks in that its glamor plays quite literally with the visible and invisible. The bikini not only makes flesh visible but it also toys with the invisible. A fabric of gravid suspension, it gestures to fertility, to family. Playing on the biblical sense of to know, Merleau-Ponty speaks of the spousal look: "The look, we said, envelops, palpates, espouses the visible things. As though it were in a relation of pre-established harmony with them, as though it knew them before knowing them" (*VI*, 133). The hand that touches "espouses" (*VI*, 141[21]) the world, with family the undertow of marriage and body: "If it touches them and sees them, this is only because, being of their family, itself visible and tangible, it uses its own being as a means to participate in theirs, because each of the two beings is an archetype for the other" (*VI*, 137).

Merleau-Ponty has recourse to marriage and family to explain concrete experience—a mind filled with discrete object-contents. It is to these institutions that Merleau-Ponty turns to explain the pre-established harmony of world and mind, to explain how it is that I experience and act on the world at all. Experience and action bow to pregnancy; my sovereignty is invaginated because marriage and family are establishment writ into flesh. Speech puts its seal on pregnancy (mind and world), but in speech (action), the subject "also sets himself up as *delocutary*, speech of which one speaks: he offers himself and offers every word to a universal

Word" (*VI,* 154). Pregnancy is always seminal, compelling: the gardener is deferential to "the living plant." The rituals of gardening obey "that λoΥoς that pronounces itself silently in each sensible thing, inasmuch as it varies around a certain type of message, which we can have an idea of only through our carnal participation in its sense, only by espousing by our body its manner of 'signifying'—or of that λoΥoς uttered whose internal structure sublimates our carnal relation with the world" (*VI,* 208).

As Kolnai points out, philosophical positions ultimately come down to where the emphasis is placed, and this chapter closes with Merleau-Ponty, a moderate realist, putting emphasis on a meaningful world (value tones) to which we and establishment witness and give testimony (*AE,* 161). Indeed, we and establishment are flesh, a doubling: whether we are in black tie at the opera or playing on the beach in a bikini, our lives are in a posture of distance, liturgical.

VALUE THEORY AND NATURAL LAW

Przywara is especially worried by the human tendency to pacify God, to think of God as something like an unproblematic, close friend. He makes clear that there is no warrant for such an idea scripturally or philosophically and, indeed, the case is rather the reverse. Many biblical texts—and not only the book of Job—speak of an uncanny God, a God who allots fate and leads souls into and out of the underworld (*AE,* 413–14, 496, 547–48).

Whenever Przywara speaks of God as uncanny, he also speaks of God behind a curtain or peering through a "gentle veil" (*AE,* 274, 284). During Holy Week, God is at his most uncanny, the Father exposing the Son to the malice of demons and men. Ritually, in Catholic churches, this strangeness is marked by purple cloth veiling crosses. It is a way for the church to shield us from God's most awful incomprehensibility: "he who became accursed is the blessing of God" (*AE,* 548).

This problematic, indeed terrifying, intimacy and distance ("a quaking ground" [*AE,* 209]) expresses Lateran IV's "ever greater." Claude Lefort's failure to observe this wrecks havoc with his work. He argues that Stalinism and Nazism are theologies because they are governed by the image of organic community, "the image of a society which is at one with itself and which has mastered its history."[1] My discussion of Kolnai's *The War against the West* in chapter 4 showed that Nazism is far stranger than this, but the main point is that Lefort is analytically wrong: Catholic political theology does not drive at the univocity of organic community. In fairness to Lefort, Kolnai, in 1934 essays, documents some Fascist Catholics who did imagine a univocal politics,[2] but it is clear Przywara would have no truck with such (*AE*, xxii, 177, 183–84). The "posture of distance" prevents any ambition to master God and map him directly onto society. This is why natural law is also called the "law of liberty" (Francisco de Vitoria). No mastery of God is possible, for God plays with us, says Aquinas: "Deus *subterfugit* formam intellectus nostri quasi omnem formam intellectus nostri excedens" (*AE*, 290; emphasis mine). If Stalinism and Nazism are theologies, they are heresies that in fact track a metaphysical decapitation under press from Parmenides and Heraclitus, as I showed in the introduction.

Lefort thinks that a healthy body politics is one that models Merleau-Ponty's splitting or doubling flesh: it blocks any politics seeking an image identical to itself in society. I argued in *Ecstatic Morality and Sexual Politics* that Wojtyla makes a distinctive contribution to natural law thinking by identifying that, in Thomas, law is linked with a wound of love.[3] Natural law is the body as dehiscence—flesh splitting in acts of generosity. Interested readers can look at *Ecstatic Morality*, but here I reformulate its central claim that the rule of law is writ in our bodies, for our flesh is ecstatic, always playfully and ritually bowing to value tones.[4] Przywara agrees with Lefort (and Agamben) that the managerial state is pernicious: it stems from a decapitation and usurps popular sovereignty writ in the festive body, thus running counter to natural law as the "law of liberty." Yet how is natural law the root of a festive body? Aren't the commandments killjoys? Isn't Christ a bit of a scold at the end of the day?

Thomas Aquinas writes, "The Old Law was not only that of the Father, but also that of the Son, because Christ was prefigured in the Old Law; for this reason the Lord says: 'If you believed Moses, you would also believe me; for he wrote about me'" (*ST* I–II, q. 106, a. 4, ad 3; cf. John 14:9; *AE*, 532–33). In his 1993 encyclical, John Paul II writes, "These [attributes of human flourishing] are the goods safeguarded by the commandments, which, according to Saint Thomas, contain the whole natural law."[5] Together, these two quotes generate the following claim: natural law is the Ten Commandments, and natural law expresses Christ.

What problem does natural law, so understood, solve? Similar to Benedict, John Paul II knew *AE*, which shaped *Veritatis Splendor*. The pope argues that people today justify their moral actions by flipping between vitalism and angelism. Relying on vitalism, people explain their acts with phrases like "we're hard-wired" or "I cannot help myself" or "it's better than repressing." People happily flip from this instinctualism or natural determinism to angelism, a self-conception according to which the person is pure spirit, having complete freedom, which is sometimes expressed as "I bow my head to no one" or, cuing Mylie Cyrus, "it's my mouth, I'll say what I want to." Both statements rely on decapitation. Pope John Paul II would say that in the first, we are bodies without heads, while in the second, we are heads without bodies (*VS,* para. 46). In the first, we think we are mere bodies, inclinations, appetites, or desire (vitalism). In the second, we are only a head, our reason a sovereign domain of self-control, personal self-determination, or untroubled consent.

John Paul II, similar to Merleau-Ponty, insists we have a bodily psychology—flesh and reason—with the visible and invisible linked in moral life. Humans share a set of rational bodily desires, and, Catholic theoreticians argue, our desire is linked to God through our reason: "It also becomes clear why this law is called the natural law: it receives this name not because it refers to the nature of irrational beings but *because the reason which promulgates it is proper to human nature*" (*VS,* para. 42; emphasis mine). This quote revisited: God's reason promulgates the law, and human nature is somewhat like (analogical to) God's reason.

Our reason is like God's, and because we are creatures of rational desire, our desire is like God, too. Our rational desire is embodied, so our bodies are somewhat divinelike, being expressive of law. "The person, by the light of reason and the support of virtue, discovers in the body *the anticipatory signs*, the expression and the promise of the gift of self, in conformity with the wise plan of the Creator" (*VS,* para. 48; emphasis mine).

John Paul II argues that the Ten Commandments structure our embodied psychology as generous, social, and gracious. My gloss is that the anticipatory signs of the law (echo of Merleau-Ponty) are gesture, play, and ritual (posture) responsive and bowing to value tones (distance). Hence, following the precepts of the natural law, "in order to perfect himself in his specific order, the person must do good and avoid evil, be concerned for the transmission and preservation of life, refine and develop the riches of the material world, cultivate social life, seek truth, practice good and contemplate beauty" (*VS*, para. 51).

These moral obligations are binding on all (space), always (time): they are unchanging because the law is ultimately Christ, "who is the same yesterday and today and for ever" (*Gaudium et spes*, para. 84; cited in *VS*, para. 53). The old name for the natural law was, as de Vitoria tells us, the "law of liberty." I discuss this more later, but mindful of Lefort's error, I will add that the old name tries to capture the shyness necessary (*AE*, 413) to any theorizing about the Eternal Gardener (Dante). Put differently, the "anticipatory signs" are uniform, but establishment in which our play and ritual are expressed is varied and complex, albeit coherent.

Caution observed, do we find in the body "anticipatory signs" of the Ten Commandments? As a reminder, the commandments are:

1. I am the Lord your God: you shall not have strange Gods before me.
2. You shall not take the name of the Lord your God in vain.
3. Remember to keep holy the Lord's Day.
4. Honor your father and your mother.
5. You shall not kill.
6. You shall not commit adultery.
7. You shall not steal.
8. You shall not bear false witness against your neighbor.
9. You shall not covet your neighbor's wife.
10. You shall not covet your neighbor's goods.

The anticipatory signs in the human body include

Upright posture and capacity to bend the knee (1 and 3),
Vulnerability (5),
Physical actions connected to property (7 and 10),
Bodily heritage (4),
Sexuality (6 and 9),
Hand to heart or other gestures of trust and fidelity (2 and 8)

Mapping onto these embodiments are clothes with specific meanings. In the same order, these are

Liturgical;

Armor and camo;

Adornments and luxury;

Tribal and national costume and beloved inherited pieces;

Modest *and* erotic wear;

Uniforms of public authority, service, and sports teams

More examples could be given, but broad categories of clothing with which peoples globally are familiar track the obligations of the Ten Commandments. Is it any wonder that Merleau-Ponty's phenomenology of the body is a clothed body?

In the last chapter, we discussed the urgent problem of vanity in the West. The idea that our playclothes and liturgical dress ups defer to value tones, and as a consequence we are naturally obedient to God, is vulnerable to the charge of idolatry. The charge comes from a number of quarters. Robert Kilwardby does not accept that our bodies convey Christ. For him, Thomistic naturalism is presumption. Centuries later, Karl Barth repeats Robert's charge (discussed in chapter 1). Unease with Thomas's confidence seems implicit in the Islamic demand for "modest wear" (discussed in chapter 6). This unease expresses a doubt that natural law is a proper accounting of law and ethics (discussed in the preface and introduction). In relationship to Jewish thought, Leon Kass repeats this worry in his treatment of the Ten Commandments. For him, the Ten Commandments are a divine *correction* of human veneration. The angelism implicit in each of the above is captured in the charge of idolatry; vitalism and naturalism cannot supply images of the divine. However, in a striking move, Aquinas confronts the charge of idolatry by defending the role clothes play in the recognition of the rule of law.

I like working on classic cars, but when I get out of my depth, I visit a local car mechanic's garage in Baltimore. As you approach the door to enter the building, stretched across the window is a poster, reading "First God gave the Ten Commandments / Then came the Second Amendment."[6] It might seem strange to say, but intellectually it is a rich poster. Consider how differently Thomas Aquinas and Leon Kass would likely read it. Thomas would have found it very logical. First, the natural law and second, the human positive law. In Aquinas, civil law—human positive law—is secondary to, and bound by, natural law. If Kass were to read it, he'd find it very logical, too. First, divine positive law and second, human positive law. What's the difference? Kass stresses the sovereignty of God, with the Ten Commandments as the root of a particular *people*—the cornerstone for the building of a unique and specific *culture*. This is a possible position if the Ten Commandments are not natural law precepts that are universally comprehensible and binding on all but the formula for a *decision* made by God for a specific people.

If the Ten Commandments are a positive law made by a sovereign God, then an illustration of the standing, and grip, of this law might be the following: you are bound in a specific way to the American Founders, who posited an American way of law and life, and I am bound differently to a body of British law posited by monarchs and parliament. Is this difference between natural law (Aquinas) and divine positive law (Kass) significant? Very.

In *Veritatis Splendor*, St. John Paul II quotes Aquinas that "God gave this light and this law to man at creation" and then himself adds, that "he also did so *in the history of* Israel, particularly in the "ten words," *the commandments of Sinai.*" (quoted in *VS*, para. 12; emphasis original). In Thomas's account, natural law was not promulgated in history but was rather promulgated with rationality itself (*ST* I–II, q. 100, a. 3).[7] What is the deep reason Aquinas and John Paul II think the Decalogue—"God's original plan for mankind" (*VS*, para. 22)—was given with creation itself? Francisco de Vitoria provides a vivid answer: "A doubt arises whether it would not be enough for all human law to derive from positive law? What need is there for it to derive from natural law? The reply to this is that even positive divine law itself is to a certain degree dependent on natural law, because God 'ordereth all things graciously' (Wisd. 8:1). Hence there has never been a divine law which did not have some reason in natural law."[8]

This is a tremendously rich and significant comment by de Vitoria. A bit later, we will examine its stress on graciousness as an objective moral and aesthetic reality that God deploys in creation. First, though, we will pause and note that de Vitoria upends the common division of the Decalogue into two tables. The first table regards duties to God and is typically thought to be divine positive law. The second concerns duties to one's neighbor and is often treated as natural law. Kass says at one point that the second table concerns eternal and absolute moral norms. This sounds like natural law, though in conversation, Kass hesitated to agree.[9]

Do the tables have different moral standing? Along with de Vitoria, Aquinas thinks not. Aquinas argues that the Decalogue is all natural law. St. John Paul II speaks of two tables but argues they are ultimately one, "acknowledging the Lord as God is the very core, the heart of the Law, from which the particular precepts flow and towards which they are ordered" (VS, 11). And so Aquinas argues that keeping the Sabbath is "in conformity to right reason,"[10] since in seeking God—a basic rational inclination, thinks Aquinas—time must be set aside to be mindful of God (ST I–II, q. 100, a. 3, ad 2).

If there is no distinction between them in moral ontology, the two tables do express noetic differences. But even here an interesting dispute opens between Aquinas and Kass. The force of some precepts, natural reason "of its own accord and at once" recognizes. These include "do not kill," "do not steal" *and* "honor thy father and mother." Others require instruction by the wise, and some, such as the prohibition against idols, require instruction by God (ST I–II, q.100, a.1). We are especially interested in this last.

Aquinas puts honoring mother and father alongside the precepts of the second table as precepts evident to unaided reason.[11] One reason is because he thinks that being kind to benefactors is evident through natural reason (ST I–II, q. 11, a. 5, ad 4). Kass disputes this and offers the compelling observation that our civilization, as shaped by the Bible, takes honoring mother and father for granted but thinks this is surely not the natural way of the world. He notes that the natural family is oftentimes a nursery of rivalry and iniquity, including incest and patricide, and cultures often honor heroes and leaders more than parents. This is a rich dispute between Aquinas and Kass, but we might note that Dante, for example, follows Aquinas. He argues that a particularly bad spot is reserved in hell for those who betray benefactors.[12]

Kass highlights the Decalogue's great opening, and the stark contrast between being with the Lord or being in "the house of bondage" (Exod. 20:2). This recalls the claim of Max Scheler that you must worship either the Christian God or some other one, and the latter is bound to be much less nice. Following from this, Kass makes a striking point about Exodus 20:3, which reads, "Thou shalt not have other [or "strange"; *aherim*] gods before Me." Kass renders this prohibition not as a declaration of philosophical monotheism but of *cultural* monotheism. I love this point. It is a claim about cultural monotheism because strange gods (Exod. 20:3) are linked to a prohibition of idols (Exod. 20:4); thus, it foregrounds the connection between religion and veneration. The essential difference, thinks Kass, between the Lord and strange gods is that no god but the Lord can furnish the world with grace, kindness, and blessing.

Kass translates the Hebrew *hesed* as *grace,* but, unlike the Latin *gratia,* the Hebrew does not appear to have any link to poise. I am no Hebrew scholar, but a survey of sources does not pick out a connection, as there is in Latin, to aesthetics. In conversation, Kass granted this difference. Grace has a bond with poise, and with what is becoming and comely, because *gratia* has its root in *gratus,* meaning *pleasing.* Interestingly, the Greek and Latin translations of the Hebrew Bible translate *hesed* as mercy (*eleos* and *misericordia,* respectively).

The Hebrew gives the religious a moral rather than an aesthetic tone. Kass argues that in Israel, what is made holy is not a special object, place, or practice but the time of your life. We might say something complex and abstract, rather than geographical. This is repeated in devotion. About the Sabbath in the Decalogue, Kass notes that no rituals or sacrifices are specified and that what is requisite is an absence, a cessation, a desisting. Of course, rituals and sacrifices will later be specified, but for the Decalogue, what is most basic is affirming that the Sabbath is a call to remember that what has often been widely worshipped—heaven, earth, sea, and all they contain—is not divine.

It is crucial to remember that this is a matter of stress or emphasis, for as Kass points out, earlier, in the book of Genesis, the majesty and goodness of creation are affirmed. Still, the stress on univocity is there, and thus in Exodus 20:23, the prohibition against idols is reaffirmed. Permission is given to have an altar of earth, but there is a prohibition against not a stone altar but one of "hewn stone:" "for if thou lift up thy tool upon it, thou hast polluted it" (Exod. 20:25).

Kass gives five arguments against representing God in images. These are 1) worshipping *things* demeans *persons*; 2) natural things are not salvific;

3) crafting images of the divine is presumption, for the principle of se-
lection assumes a false intimacy; 4) sophisticated idols can seduce us into
venerating their makers; and, finally, 5) idols inherently celebrate human
artfulness and thus necessarily obscure the reality of pervasive human
twistedness. In his treatment of idolatry, Aquinas picks up on this dark-
ness, noting that idolatry frequently involves the evils of mutilation and
homicide (*ST* II–II, q. 94, a. 4, ad. 1). (I discuss natural law and Thomas
on the rule of homicide elsewhere.) However, as a follower of Anselmian
humanism and defender of the *analogia entis* formulated at Lateran IV,
Thomas affirms that human craft can properly render the "posture of
distance."

Aquinas argues that the Decalogue offers cautions about images rather
than strict prohibitions (*ST* I–II, q. 100, a. 4). Aquinas's epistemology
begins from the senses, and religion and faith are no exceptions. We first
encounter the divine in sacrifices and games (*ST* II–II, q. 94, a. 1), he argues, not in the "pure mind" (*ST* II–II, q. 94, a. 2). Citing Aristotle's *Po-
etics*, Thomas notes that humans have a natural delight in representations
(*ST* II–II, q. 94, a. 4) but, following both Aristotle and Basil, Aquinas
insists that the honor given to an image reaches to its prototype (*ST* III,
q. 25, a. 3). Here are two striking comments from Thomas (*ST* III, q. 25,
a. 2): "To adore the flesh of Christ is nothing else than to adore the incarnate Word of God: just as to adore a King's robe is nothing else than to
adore a robed King. And in this sense the adoration of Christ's humanity is
the adoration of 'latria.'" And "no honour or reverence is due save by reason of a rational nature. And this in two ways. First, inasmuch as it represents a rational nature: secondly, inasmuch as it is united to it in any way
whatsoever. In the first way men are wont to venerate the king's image; in
the second way, his robe. And both are venerated by men with the same
veneration as they show to the king."

Thomas is in that long line of thinkers stretching from Plato to
Shaftesbury to Kolnai who think in terms of ascending scales of graciousness and participation, with the physical lifted and made glamorous and
luminous by its being expressive of that which is prior and higher and,
in the case of a monotheistic metaphysics, personal. Aquinas argues that
fine clothing, far from being an impediment to worship of God, helps
elevate our minds to God: "Now in order that any man may dwell aright

in a community, two things are required: the first is that he behave well
to the head of the community; the other is that he behave well to those
who are his fellows and partners in the community. It is therefore necessary that the Divine law should contain in the first place precepts ordering man in his relations to God; and in the second place, other precepts
ordering man in his relations to other men who are his neighbors and
live with him under God" (*ST* I–II, q. 100, a. 5).

The veneration of the robes of kings and queens is analogous to the
veneration of religious statues and relics, and both are deferential gestures
upward to offices and persons exceeding their embodiments in artifacts.
Establishment is Burke's term, but in Aquinas, it is to record that human
being is an obediential potency (*potentia obedientialis*) to a sacral universe
(*AE,* xxiii, 306). There can be strange gods, but not every artifact imag-
ing God counts as a strange god. God creates out of graciousness and
this objective ethical and aesthetic fund furnishes a sacral universe natural and artifactual. How does one identify a strange god? Put differently,
what counts as immoral veneration?

"Whom are you wearing tonight: Dolce and Gabbana, Victoria Beck-
ham, or Alexander McQueen?" The beaux often ask each other this sort of
question. Thanks to the entrepreneurial spirit of a recent college graduate,
an answer in the future might be "McQueen, literally."

London's famous fashion school Central Saint Martins graduated a
designer last year with a highly original idea that is justly garnering press
coverage. Tina Gorjanc has cleverly updated the idea of the reliquary.[13]
She is seeking patents for a lab procedure that will enable her to take a
deceased person's DNA and cultivate the person's skin. The procedure is
known as de-extinction, and her concept is to take the DNA of the brilliant but troubled British designer Alexander McQueen (1969–2010)
and make jackets and handbags using his skin.

Business ethics tries to discern the moral reasons obliging a business to leave money on the table: to clarify the reasons why, despite willing buyers and legal freedom to make a contract, a business still ought
to walk away from a sale or deal. Is a jacket made from Alexander Mc-
Queen a case in point? McQueen committed suicide in 2010 but was
already highly acclaimed, not least for his varied meditations on embodiment. For this reason, Gorjanc is likely right when she says he'd surely

approve of her business proposal. A warning flag might be that other objects made of human skin are often linked to punishment. John Horwood was executed in Bristol in 1821 for the bludgeoning to death of Eliza Balsum. After he died on the gallows, the surgeon Richard Smith dissected Horwood's body at Bristol's Royal Infirmary as part of a public lecture. Smith later wrote a book about the murder and dissection and used Horwood's skin to cover the book.[14] Far earlier in English history, the door to Worcester Cathedral was covered in the skin of a Viking, who was flayed for trying to steal a church bell.[15]

Learning of Gorjanc's concept, people express disgust and make mention of *Silence of the Lambs* and the "Witch of Buchenwald," Ilse Koch. Disgust is an anchor of moral order, a sure sign that something is amiss. It also has a definite structure. Precisely why a McQueen jacket provokes disgust is a little difficult to pin down.

Excarnation was a practice in the Middle Ages making possible the veneration of saints: specifically, the veneration of the body parts of saints. The practice involved boiling the flesh off the bones of the dead (this was the fate of Aquinas's body). When the dead person was thought saintly, the bones would be broken up, put in reliquaries, and dispatched throughout Europe for veneration. Indeed, money was to be made, and trade in reliquaries thrived. Are we just more squeamish than the medievals?

Is an important difference between the medieval and contemporary reliquary that the former (mostly) displayed bone? Is the hardness of bone inherently different from the suppleness of skin? In his seminal work *On Disgust*, Aurel Kolnai identifies slime, viscosity, and stickiness as leading qualities of the disgusting.[16] Catholicism is no stranger to the ghoulish, but it was thought a bridge too far when a Polish cardinal kept vials of blood after John Paul II was treated at Gamelli hospital. However, Gorjanc's mock-ups of the clothes and accessories she plans to make with McQueen's skin—the mock-ups are made of animal skins—have all the polish of luxury goods.

Kolnai also identifies the way that the disgusting reaches out to us, as it were: our sense that the disgusting probes us oftentimes provokes retching, as if we wanted to put distance between it and ourselves. The suppleness of skin suggests something "breathing," alive almost, agile—so alive that Gorjanc touts as an interesting style feature that the jackets will tan in the sun at different rates, adding to each a unique and exclusive quality. Indeed, she sees no reason why owners couldn't tattoo the skin. The disgust reaction to Gorjanc's concept might be rooted in an obtrusive intimacy that is built into the jackets, but from time immemorial, humans have worn animal skins and even displayed battle trophies: heads on spikes, scalps, and shrunken heads dangling from belts. *Game of Thrones* has put all this vividly back into our minds. Justice itself has long been connected to body parts—see Ian Miller's fantastic philosophy of law book *An Eye for an Eye*—and there is some evidence that early forms of money were made up of body parts.[17] And yet I think there is something about the obtrusiveness of Gorjanc's planned reliquaries that makes them problematic. It lacks discretion.

We respect persons because their attributes are valuable: persons are original and are creative centers of imagination, speech, play, and ideas. Persons demand justice because they are self-contained, discerning, and capable of self-regulation. By contrast, the disgusting is sticky, smearing, and as Kolnai puts it, smirking and leering. Disgust is a moral disvalue because it intrudes on and subverts what is valuable about persons: it aims to cover-up what is original and remove value from the world. The disgusting is the inverse of a "posture of distance."

While a jacket made of the skin of Alexander McQueen—cultivated in a lab, with the property relations of DNA murky—might not be Alexander McQueen himself, nonetheless that skin is *his*. This means when an Alexander McQueen skin jacket is worn in the street, McQueen in some manner will leap about between persons. His will be a "life out of place." Just as I can intrude inappropriately in your life, McQueen will seem to intrude when and if you and I rub shoulders with his skin. Odd as it is to say, medieval veneration was more discreet, more respectful of persons.

Part of what seems wrong about this is the idea that McQueen deserves rest. Gorjanc is giving to McQueen an afterlife, but our sense of the afterlife is clearly expressed in our hope that the dead will rest in peace. No life escapes trouble and burden—and McQueen's life was more troubled than many—and a consolation of death is the hope of peaceful rest. Medieval reliquaries are lodged in chapels; they are resting places for saints. Is our moral reservation about Gorjanc's innovation that she will burden McQueen by making him continue to flit across our streets?

Gorjanc may see this herself. She has suggested that the McQueen garments will be installed in art museums. She intuits McQueen ought to have his resting place. Her entrepreneurship is directed primarily at helping the fashion industry find ways to generate animal skins in a cruelty-free way, and her patents for de-extinction have this business goal primarily in mind. This part of her business plan seems unproblematic, and hopefully her ingenuity will be rewarded. Some dress ups fail to express the "posture of distance" that is the inner structure of natural law, itself an expression of *analogia entis* and the true metaphysics of morals.

CHAPTER EIGHT

PLAY AND LITURGY

Written in 1947, Albert Camus's *The Plague* imagines a modern unexceptional city succumbing to the bubonic plague. It is a riveting story and opens cinematically: as a doctor leaves his apartment for work one morning, he sees a dead rat lying on one of the front steps. Puzzled, but not overly, he sidesteps the rat and goes about his day. The doctor's everyday circumstances are about to change utterly.

Camus's novel addresses the existential and political consequences of a collapse in normal circumstances: whole families rapidly fall to the plague, soldiers ring the city, organized crime turns to running the blockade, and burying the dead becomes perfunctory. Interestingly, Camus portrays the doctors as hated figures, since their arrival at a home means families will be split up, the sick moved to a hospital to die alone, and other family members put in quarantine.

Dramatizations of people trying to cope with the collapse of everyday life now fill our screens. Films that quickly come to mind are *I Am Legend* and the Brad Pitt vehicle *World War Z*. Among TV series are *Lost*, *Battlestar Galactica*, *The Leftovers*, *Fortitude*, and *The Walking Dead*. Then there are the white walkers in *Game of Thrones*, whose arrival is foreshadowed by Ned Stark's warning "winter is coming."

Since World War II, no catastrophic event in the West has upset our everyday patterns. Some wonder whether mass migration might trigger a break in the everyday. Walter Russell Mead ponders the end of normal circumstances.[1] He astutely observes that European governments view asylum as a legal rather than as a political question. For the governments of Europe, the law demands that displaced persons have asylum. To many European peoples, the matter is not so obvious, and Mead wonders at what point "the political system will no longer carry out the legal mandate." Agamben agrees with Mead that the West is in crisis because its governments address every problem with yet more laws that suspend popular sovereignty.[2] Schmitt looms so large in his work because it is Schmitt who so clearly observed modernity's effort to obscure the political ground of legality.

Carl Schmitt (1888–1985) is best known for his theory of politics in abnormal circumstances. Thought by many to be the most profound work of political theory in the twentieth century, his *The Concept of the Political* gives the analytics of such a politics.[3] Schmitt's book dates to that dark year 1933, and thinkers like Kolnai and Johan Huizinga (1872–1945) did not think that mere coincidence. Arguably, Carl Schmitt is the most important legal and political thinker of the twentieth century, and he and Przywara knew one another. Central to Schmitt is his philosophy of the decision. His detailed historical and theoretical works show that the liberal philosophical dream that the rule of law can exclude any persons ruling other persons is false. Politics demands decision—namely, instances when some persons rule over others and, on occasion, risk those persons' lives.

In his brilliant *Homo Ludens* (1939), Huizinga picks out Schmitt's claim that abnormal circumstances must be understood as a serious emergency (*Ernstfall*), with decision the only means of resolving the emergency.[4] Huizinga turns this central claim upside down, arguing that only the playful is adequate to abnormal situations, for the ludic is the soil of civilization. It might seem strange to respond to the dire with playfulness, but Huizinga ranges across art, poetry, philosophy, politics, fashion, war, and diplomacy to demonstrate that the ludic makes civilizations resilient. Though he gives a different solution, he does agree with Schmitt that Europe's humanitarianism is not adequate to the crisis of the West. Europe's humanitarian sensibility—earnest, liberal, and secular; the champion of individual self-expression; and a weird amalgam of Romanticism and the valorization of the technological—cannot deliver a humanistic peace. Only Europe's archaic heritage, redolent with play motifs, is equal to the task. In a remarkable history of play, Huizinga identifies what he calls the "magic circle of play" in religion, politics, and commerce: things solemnly rejected by humanitarianism.

Earlier I wrote, "Christ, an offering metaphysical, the very order of natural law" is liturgy (Heb. 8:2–6).[5] Przywara, drawing on scripture, offers "the round dance of the nuptial union" as an image of the Mass (*AE,* 577). Liturgy is play, something common to animals and humans: humans and animals disport in ways ceremonious, graceful, and becoming (*AE,* 286–87, 533). Rules are obeyed, and the game is graced by value tones conveyed by establishment. Przywara points out that both Plato and Aristotle thought the consummation of philosophy was mystery and funeral rites (*AE,* 161–62). As a portrait of natural law, let's look at James Bond.

In fantasy, Bond is the answer to abnormal circumstances: he has a license to kill the enemies of the queen. His is a serious commission: defeat criminal masterminds intent on subverting the rule of law. Why then the drollery and one-liners? Are the playful elements of Bond mere entertainment, ancillary to the serious core of fighting subversion?

Among the seminal books generated by the Scottish Enlightenment is Adam Ferguson's work of political anthropology *An Essay on the History of Civil Society* (1767).[6] Containing many gems, the book highlights a demonstration that the fables and romances a civilization uses to entertain can have dramatic impact on its mores. Ferguson (1723–1816) shows that the medieval literary ideal of the knight transformed both the practice and manners of war. The Middle Ages gave us James Bond.

Before this ideal, Ferguson contends, war was typically a matter of ambush, revenge killings, and desire for spoils. No distinction was made between combatants and noncombatants, and defeat meant death or slavery. Medieval romances demanded gallantry from a knight, and slowly but surely the real expectations of soldiers changed. The refinement and courtesy of officers, indifference to spoils, a fair fight, leniency to those who surrender, and a rigorous isolation of women and children from reprisal all became part of the just conduct of war.[7] All of us can come up with examples of when soldiers failed the ideal, but cynicism might also falsify the historical record.[8]

Ferguson identifies three cultural tributaries for the knight's gallantry. The Celts contributed the formalities of the duel and the idea of combat as juridical. The Germanic tribes twinned war with a veneration of women, believing female gods, the Valkyries, would decide the outcome (*AE,* 491). Christianity contributed obedience to the rule of humble service to neighbor (*AE,* 425, 489). The result was "the hero of modern romance professes a contempt of stratagem, as well as of danger, and unites in the same person, characters and dispositions seemingly opposite; ferocity with gentleness, and the love of blood with sentiments of tenderness and pity."[9]

Ferguson is unusual as a thinker in emphasizing the role of games and play in civilization. Chaplain to the Scottish regiment of the Black Watch, Ferguson was a great admirer of the Celtic mores he observed in his soldiers. Duels and judicial combat ooze a sense of the ludic and perfectly capture Ferguson's fellow countryman James Bond. Glib one-liners dripping off his tongue, the Swiss-Scottish Bond has "a contempt of stratagem."[10] As befits a commander in the Royal Navy, Bond lives by Lord Nelson's advice, "just go straight at 'em." One for sauntering into the enemy's lair, impeccably dressed, Bond likes to challenge others to a duel. This is explicit in *The Man with the Golden Gun,* in which Moore's Bond and Scaramanga literally duel. They play a game of hide and seek among illusion-generating mirrors; the game begins with pistols drawn and twenty paces walked.

Play conveys the rule of law. Lawyers rhetorically duel and joust, following rules of procedure, and should the situation require it, they meet at the court, where pleas (derived from the Anglo-French word *plai,* meaning to braid or plait) are submitted to a judge in costume and oftentimes wearing a wig, who umpires the gamesmanship. Little wonder then that Bond responds to those seeking to subvert rule of law with a vigorous assertion of play. What better way to deflate the spoilsport than to reassert the ludic roots of law?

A court of law is like a playing field, a space where rules and outcomes are decided. Contempt of court tells participants what is out of bounds, just as certainly as the throw-in and goal kick do. Bond has a number of choice playing fields. We first meet Bond in *Dr. No* at the roulette table. Winning against a beautiful woman, Bond is all charm, as keen as any ancient German to keep the female gods on his side. No hard feelings at money lost, she leaves the table with Bond, who promptly asks, "Do you play any other games?"

As every Bond fan knows, Bond's favorite game is, in fact, motor rallying. The racetracks might be the Grand Bazaar in Istanbul or the streets of Rome, but speed racing, whether motor bikes, power boats, or even parkour, is a Bond perennial. The cars involved—the British marques, the Lotus, the Jaguar, the Aston Martin, and the delicious Sunbeam Alpine—are not accidental.

Court cases, similar to war, and games generally, are agonistic. Sides are taken, and teams and clubs are formed. Participants and spectators alike dress up in team colors, sport a sigil, or invoke ritual. New Zealand's national rugby team, All Blacks, is famous for its Maori war dance before games. Games can be bloody and damaging: boxing and fox hunting get bloody, and court cases can damage reputations forever. Bond's famous gentlemanly style shows he is on the side of establishment forces. Cinematic shots of London's governmental buildings with Bond in Savile Row tailoring are common and contrast with the underground lairs of the masterminds of the secret society Spectre. One of the most iconic scenes has Bond skiing off a mountain cliff, surely doomed, only to have a Union Jack parachute open up. Bond flies the flag.

Bond is always sporting. His British sports car the Aston Martin is part of his team colors—moviegoers literally cheered at the sight of the vintage DB6 when it reappeared in *Skyfall*—and it, too, is part of the game. The work of Q, the car performs dummies, foxing the enemy with trick features like ejector seats. Most famous of all, though, is the Lotus driven by Roger Moore's Bond, which saves Bond's bacon by converting from sports car to submarine and back again!

Less theatrical than the foppish Bond of Sir Roger Moore, the brutalist Bond of Daniel Craig still offers a fair fight. Craig's arrival in the role began famously with a "horror of war" scene: Bond and his adversary, both badly dressed and rumpled, confront each other in a raw physical struggle stripped of all glamor. The setting, irony laid on thick, is the gents. Finally gaining an advantage, Bond pushes the man's head into a toilet sink in a men's lavatory to drown him. It's a "fair fight" that could have gone the other way, with Bond dead. He has no special toys from Q to eke out an advantage. Indeed, Bond almost dies, as the man being drowned plays a dummy and fakes his death. Bond, tricked, turns his back, only for his adversary to seek out a gun. With the villain aiming at Bond's back, the scene

ends with Bond's signature swivel round shot. Even a blaggard gets a sporting chance; everyone gets to play the zealous advocate.

Despite the brawn and chip-on-the-shoulder aggression of Craig's
Bond, the Connery incarnation is more sinister. The Scottish Connery
takes to heart Ferguson's "ferocity and gentleness." The almost lullaby
quality of Connery's accented speech cannot hide his chilly indifference
when killing. Some have noted that Connery moves like a big cat, power
elegantly on display, but he also shares a cat's cold amusement with tor-
menting its prey. In the well-known scene from *Dr. No,* the first and
most iconic of all the films, Bond kills Professor Dent. Pretending not
to notice Dent going for a gun, and watching the professor's excitement
mount at possibly killing a British secret agent, Bond coldly dispatches
him at his enemy's peak moment of excitement.

But Dent, as the phrase goes, "had it coming to him." He may be
a professor, but he is also willing to have others unjustly gunned down.
Bond also represents the cold part of justice—no matter that his combat
is redolent with the themes of play, which in fact sustain the rule of law.
A creation of the West's knightly tradition, the gentlemanly knight holding the abnormal at bay so that normal life continues, has universal appeal. The Bond brand continues to grow.

Play is not thematized as such in *AE,* though play between suspended
elements (between essence and existence, between philosophy and theology, or the "interplay" between the Platonic and Aristotelian emphases,
for example) is mentioned (*AE,* 128, 207–8, 241). To a priest, the theme
is obvious. Aquinas says we come to God through play (*ST* II–II, q. 94,
a. 1): at the Mass, the priest role-plays Jesus at the Last Supper. Dressed
up in costume, the priest makes elegant ritual gestures. Accompanied
by song, these gestures happen in a space and a time set apart for the
spectacle. The aesthetics of the event are not much different from a soccer match. Of a Saturday, hallowed fields like Anfield Stadium, home of
Liverpool Football Club, fill with thousands of supporters dressed up in
colors, who, for a defined period of time, ritualistically gesture and sing.
Games solidify community identity.

The king had his court jester, and seldom a day goes by when we
don't marvel at the clownishness of our politicians. British prime minis-
ters win the joust that is prime minister's Question Time in Parliament if

they can transform the leader of Her Majesty's opposition into a panto-
mime villain. Laughter and jeers greet every political put-down. The en-
tertainments of Parliament are not much removed from those of a pub.
And as with pub games, political gamesmanship draws the different sides
of communities together.

Our comedy shows confirm that office life is a series of "contests,
performances, exhibitions, challenges, preenings, struttings and showing-
off, pretenses and binding rules."[11] An excellent summary of commerce as
game is offered in the super speech delivered by Jeremy Irons in *Margin
Call*, a 2011 film portraying the reckless financial gambling that gave us
the turmoil of the 2008 financial freeze. Adam Smith does not disagree.
He insists commerce functions only in light of exhibitions of wealth. Design objects and fashionable accessories are, as Adam Smith puts it, toys
and "trinkets of frivolous utility," and yet they stir the fantasies of an entire civilization.[12] Toys regenerate communities.

The West's ambition toward humanitarian universalism needs play if
its civilization is to be resilient in abnormal circumstances. Ethical formalism must be "rooted in the primaeval soil of play," and the West
must affirm rather than run from its heritage in religion, politics, and
commerce. Morals require liturgy. Just as the liturgies of the Mass and
football match happen on hallowed ground, so does legal and moral formalism need geography: there is no play without a playing field and no
playing field without a vigorous sense of place. Play "proceeds within its
own proper boundaries of time and space," and games have a tendency to
found clubs.[13] Think only of our tennis, soccer, and golf clubs, to name a
few. This being "apart together" is basic to play, but it does not mean pa-
rochialism. It means civilization.

Teams combine into leagues, into associations, and even into governing international bodies. Historically, many games have been cruel and
bloody, and Huizinga observes that war and diplomacy have the attributes of games. Sides are taken, people dress up, dummies and cheating
are attempted, and ferocity lights up the contest. However, as with all
games, there are limits. Geography shapes borders and the field of battle,
and there are long-established rules of engagement, as well as expectations
that teams will play with honor, decency, and good form and also be good
losers. Gamesmanship is expected but so too is ensuring opponents have a

sporting chance, while being a spoilsport brings opprobrium on an adversary and even nations. Despite the contest, the play forms are recognized internationally, and all communities are required to observe them or live with the consequences. Belonging does not mean tribalism.

Przywara consistently speaks of the "decisive analogy." Famously, Schmitt argues that no politics can, in principle, avoid the friend-enemy distinction and the fateful moment of decision when someone, or some group of persons, invokes it. Schmitt describes this moment in existential terms, stripped of any concrete value guidance. Przywara's "decisive analogy" is not a concept, theory, or principle but a posture (*AE,* 375). This is not existential, for posture connotes bodily habit, a certain stylized way of articulating the body. A "posture of distance" is the "decisive analogy," an obedience to "the sovereignty of the divine majesty itself" (*AE,* 375). Into Schmitt's decision, Przywara introduces deference to a ritual order beyond political order, which like all play manifests the beautiful and good.[14] Politics, similar to law, is analogical. The friend-enemy distinction is not a sui generis revelation of threat but the moment a civilization appeals to what is richest in it and uses those values to communicate with others, even if sometimes combat is necessary to impose its good and beautiful liturgies.

As in the last chapter, Kolnai's value phenomenology was used to assess rogue venerations, so natural law can assess dress ups. The corset is making a comeback. Some worry there are political implications, that corsets objectify by pushing the female body to "perverse proportions."[15] How can one assess the morality of "perverse proportions"? Natural law aims to track the natural (good) and unnatural (perverse). While the corset has been slumbering in ordinary life, in the make-believe worlds of fetish and body modification it has flourished. In those worlds, the corset is much admired for its exaggeration of form, its baroque playfulness.

One might wonder about the psychology of extreme body modifiers; surely the suspicion that they are "messed up" is never far away. However, there is no doubt that sometimes there is no psychological story to be told, for example, among tribal peoples who wear lip plates. Lip plates are totemic in some way, but they are not psychological in the contemporary Western sense. We are likely to suspect the latter is true of people like Michele Kobke.[16]

One might expect a saint of the Catholic Church to be against body modification, but, if we look at the core precepts of the Thomistic natural law, we find it offering significant latitude in this regard. As we saw in the last chapter, according to John Paul II's formulation, there are four core precepts:

1. All things seek to maintain existence,
2. All animals seek to procreate and care for the young,
3. All humans seek society and knowledge, and
4. All humans seek God.

It is fairly clear that most body modification does not touch on these core precepts. One could imagine certain body modifications damaging health and others twisting the body so as to become socially aversive, but, broadly, much body modification and corset wearing would encounter natural law as "a law of liberty"[17]—that is, with tolerance. "Perverse proportions" are surely possible but 99 percent of corset wearing likely does not qualify.

To offer a different example, are tax havens immoral?[18] They look both like a case of decapitation and like "perverse proportions" in wealth. A family (head) squirrels away wealth taken from the nation state (body) and stores it offshore. There are roughly 170,000 high-net-worth individuals globally (defined as those with at least thirty million dollars in investable assets), almost all of whom rely on tax havens to shield their wealth. Wealth managers are responsible for squirreling away the assets. A typical client is male, middle aged, has more than thirty million dollars net, and interested primarily in the conservation of his wealth and its careful distribution to family. Discretion and a strong stomach are necessary because it is remarkably common for the manager to devise disbursements for the family *and* for a second family, the secret children of a paramour. These men believe their wealth has two predators: government and spendthrift family members.

People in the West are schizophrenic about the superwealthy. We rail against tax havens yet adore celebrities, almost all of whom make eager use of them to fund the glamor we love. Leaders of tech companies and playboys, pop stars, and Hollywood leading ladies all shield wealth in tax havens and yet are beloved by the Left, who otherwise denounce the 1 percent. Just 0.7 percent of the global population owns 41 percent of assets worldwide.

Abstractly, we are stunned and mortified by that number, but as it shows itself in glamorous play, we fall under a spell.[19] We connive at the cat-and-mouse game of tax avoidance because its play motif is alluring. Sundry accountants, lawyers, opera singers, and yacht crews make up the ranks of wealth managers. Many live on the islands used for offshoring wealth: the Cook Islands, the British Virgin Islands, the Caymans, the Channel Islands, and so on. Some have the pedigree you might expect—British public school and Oxbridge—whereas others have no university education, nor is one strictly needed. Until very recently, no special training was available for becoming a wealth manager. Manchester University in England was the first to offer such a certificate, and that was in 2011. What seems to be more crucial than formal education for gaining entre into wealth management is what social theorist Pierre Bourdieu calls "social capital": graceful physical bearing, playing the right games (sport shooting and hunting, polo, and sailing), good manners, and knowledge of and ease around expensive things. Huizinga would not be remotely surprised.

Have we tools to resist the allure of play; how can we determine if this game of cat and mouse is as truly out of bounds as it is truly beyond national borders? The instruments deployed to shield wealth are philosophically interesting. The trust fund is the preferred tool—though there is a need for others because wealth and trust do not combine well in all cultures. The trust emerged in medieval England, when knights leaving for the Crusades needed to secure their families' wealth in their long years of absence campaigning. Ecclesiastical courts were distinct from the state's, and shrouding wealth in church law created onshore islands that were, so to say, independent of the Crown. Because of the pervasive reach of the modern liberal administrative state, the capacity of a trust to escape government is viewed more skeptically. The medieval onshore island has been housed mostly offshore to make doubly sure prying fingers do not succeed in raiding the family coffers: offshore islands offer very low rates of taxation, combined with vigorous impediments to legal challenges coming from abroad. The Cook Islands is one of the most remote places on earth, and, even if lawyers make it to the islands, its government boasts that it has never acceded to a legal challenge to break a trust.

The masterstroke of the concept of the trust is to transfer the wealthy person's legal ownership to a trustee, all the while ensuring that the original owner and his family are the sole recipients of the benefits of the property they relinquish into the hands of the trustee. For centuries, trustees were simply men of standing known to the family—amateurs who cautiously tended the trust with the aim of conserving rather than growing its holdings. Though trustees today are mostly professional managers, they remain committed to conserving wealth rather than risking it in potential high-return investments. Their charge is to ensure the property maintains itself and is able to make distributions for generations.

The umbrella professional association, the Society of Trust and Estate Practitioners, is based in London and was only founded in 1991. Its literature boldly affirms a strong libertarian stance that taxation is little better than thievery. This stance justifies leeching capital from nations and minimizing financial contributions to the common good. High-net-worth individuals almost always want to live in their countries of origin and thus live the highlife on the back of a common good to which they do not contribute. This might not be as morally rotten as it first appears. Burke makes the concept of the trust his guiding analogy for a healthy polity.

Burke is skeptical about a politics of innovation and change. De Tocqueville marveled that in America wealth "circulates with inconceivable rapidity," and Franklin Roosevelt lambasted "fortunes by will, inheritance, or gift" as inconsistent "with the ideals and sentiments of the American people." However, Burke compares a strident call for change and progress to the release of a volatile gas. Liberty for a mass of persons is power, he argues, and power unrestrained by the established order is bound to be abusive.[20] The trust offers the right model for combining the claims of establishment and the need for a polity to respond to historical change and new mores: "It leaves acquisition free; but it secures what it acquires. Whatever advantages are obtained by a state proceeding on these maxims, are locked fast as in a sort of family settlement; grasped as in a kind of mortmain forever. By a constitutional policy, working after the pattern of nature, we receive, we hold, we transmit our government and our privileges, in the same manner in which we enjoy and transmit our property and our lives."[21]

That is staggering, but Burke asks us to carefully consider our egalitarian intuitions. His politics, what he calls "the method of nature," is analogous to the rhythm of the family. Rather beautifully, he writes, "In this choice of inheritance we have given to our frame of polity the image of a relation of blood; binding up the constitution of our country with our dearest domestic ties; adopting our fundamental laws into the bosom of our family affections; keeping inseparable, and cherishing with the warmth of all their combined and mutually reflected charities, our state, our hearths, our sepulchres, and our altars."[22]

Rectifying the inequality of inherited money would require breaking the trust, but this would be no mere overhaul of state revenue. It would be a body blow to the family as a stabilizing and generative force in the nation (*AE*, 491) and radically advance and cement the totalizing tendency of the managerial state. In other words, not the trust itself but the breaking of the trust is a decapitation. Tax havens might not be the best things about the world, but Burke clarifies why the trust is a profound invention of the Middle Ages and one best left alone.

CONCLUSION

Moral Theory and Liturgy

From migration to the managerial state, and from robots to sumptuary laws, the West faces moral questions that all have one thing in common: decapitation. Przywara's insight into the metaphysics of morals, decapitation is the reason modernity's humanism is failing. In practice and theory, again and again, modernity offers either vitalism or angelism—sometimes both at once. Instead of providing a bodily moral psychology, modernity proffers a humanism wherein we figure either as angels or as naturalistic drives. Przywara shows that a univocal metaphysics gives angelism an equivocal vitalism. There are two ways to cast humans as godlike: by giving us either divinelike minds or bodily superpowers. Univocal and equivocal metaphysics split what needs to be held in tension.

Puzzled by the structure and change observed throughout nature, ancient metaphysicians gave priority either to structure (univocity) or to change (equivocity), and this is no mere error of the ancients. It is a recurring difficulty, repeated through the development of Western metaphysics, to find a pattern of thought able to hold the two emphases together. This pattern was finally delivered, argues Przywara, in 1215, at the Fourth Lateran Council, in its formula of analogy. Metaphysics is properly an *analogia entis.*

It is natural law that best tracks the *analogia entis*. Benthamite utilitarianism thinks ethical problems are rooted in vitalism—how to adjudicate competing drives of pleasure and pain—and proposes the yardstick of a mathematical rule.[1] It flips between vitalism and angelism, therefore. Kantian formalism (e.g., Hans Kelsen or John Rawls) is angelism,[2] relying on the most dualistic passages in Kant.[3] It ought to be noted that John Mill's utilitarianism and the Kant of *Anthropology from a Pragmatic Point of View* contain ethical insights that bring them closer to the defense of natural law offered here.

Przywara's "posture of distance" captures that being human is an expression of the *analogia entis*, an "in-and-beyond" (change and order). This posture is natural law and, as I have shown, it is far from being the desire for organic community (the fusion of life and political order, as Lefort thinks); it is, rather, ludic and tolerant. The playfulness of natural law does not exclude definite prohibitions against kinds of sexual acts (McAleer 2005), kinds of killing (McAleer 2017), kinds of social organization (McAleer 2014), or kinds of business practices (McAleer 2016).[4] Every ethical theory establishes prohibitions—that is the point, after all—but natural law is also a "law of liberty." Just as games permit dummies and cheeky plays within the rules, and even permit breaking rules with assigned penalties, so is natural law tolerant of all manner of human playfulness and enterprise. Games and natural law do not tolerate the spoilsport, however.

This tolerance extends to theorists, too. Kolnai mentioned at one point how puzzling he found Thomists, who seemed to dismiss the moral insights of other ethical theorists. One, of course, also meets rigid Kantians and Benthamites all the time. Kolnai thought Thomas Reid's moral realism was especially congruent with Catholic humanism, and I agree. Precisely how to think of natural law has always been tricky, though it is not more tricky than how precisely to understand Kant or than wrestling with the idea of happiness in utilitarianism. Common intellectual complaints against natural law are that it is biologistic, and somewhat contradictorily a priori and mechanical, and the common political complaint is that it is hostile to progressive politics and totalizing about sex and fertility.

My account of natural law is inspired by Thomas, de Vitoria, and Wojtyla, but Przywara's "posture of distance" has proved crucial in making me think about posture and gesture as primary ethical matters. This is why Reid and Merleau-Ponty figure in this book. It is also implicit in the British eighteenth-century idea of the spectator, so marvelously detailed by Adam Smith. Games are about posture and gesture—hence Huizinga's role here. As Huizinga points out, games have their rituals and liturgy. Put differently, natural law is not biologistic, a priori, and mechanical, or totalizing, because it is about gesture, games, and civilization. It is about inclinations but not naturalistic drives (vitalism), and it is about rules but not deductions from a narrow set of a priori principles (angelism).

As is evident from my arguments, ritual and liturgy display an in-and-beyond structure. We express our bodies within them and so defer to establishment. As Shaftesbury, Burke, Scheler, and Kolnai show, this deference is a bow to value tones. We are bodily the rule of law (we span vitalism and angelism). As is demonstrated by the placing of a hand over the heart, the handshake, the blood brother ritual, the Islamic footballer's prostration and the two-handed gesture to heaven on scoring, as well as by the Catholic footballer's touching the grass and making the sign of the cross on entering the field of contest, Reid's gestural body observes the decorum of the game (establishment) and is at home in and at court, on the playing field, and in the boardrooms of commerce and politics.[5]

This is confirmed from Merleau-Ponty's exploration of childhood. An infant becomes intensely social when "others" appear to the child thanks to a "postural schema," an imitative structure of an original sympathy, wherein "self" and "other" are not yet clearly demarcated.[6] This idea of an original sympathy Merleau-Ponty takes from Scheler (119), which he glosses as "wherein the other's intentions somehow play *across* my body while my intentions play across his" (119), this leads to a "postural impregnation" (118, 141). Language happens through role-play (109), and around one year of age, clarity of self and other is established. Playing in front of mirrors or practicing gestures in mirrors becomes common, and even up to nearly three years of age, children can be observed kissing their images in a mirror "very ceremoniously" (130–31).

Decorum makes prominent value tones that are part of the natural furniture of the world and give it its gloss: they are what civilization appeals to and venerates (sovereignty). In no way are these value tones the equivalent of what God is. The *analogia entis* means God is always hither *and* yonder *and* behind a veil, intimate and uncanny, but equally value tones are about God—thus Dante's beautiful name for God, Eternal Gardener. Natural law is naturalism but not vitalism. It is also not angelism, for it is a posture, an espousing bow toward fecund value tones.[7] Natural law is humanism.

Formalism in ethics mistakes what ethics is about, whereas natural law does not. Natural law is the foundation of humanism because natural law blocks decapitation. Mill's utilitarianism and Kant's ethics of the *Anthropology* edge away from decapitation somewhat, as does Smith's idea of the impartial spectator as a demigod.[8] However, Levinas suffers from angelism[9] and a typical Darwinian from vitalism.[10] Malthus inspired Darwin and is a good example of vitalism consistently applied,[11] though De Waal has shown the modesty of Darwin's own claims[12] and linked them back nicely to both Smith and Aquinas.[13] Though Mandeville's fable is one of the more ludic presentations of ethics, his egoism, expressive of "our vile tubes," is a vitalism. Lacan is anxious to avoid Freud's vitalism, and Merleau-Ponty *carefully* appropriates the link he makes between desire and rhetoric in *The Visible and the Invisible*. However, Lacan's reflections on ethics firmly invoke equivocity, the fragmentary and damaged self spinning out from "the thick absence called desire" (so redolent of Schopenhauer): "Physical reality is fully and totally inhuman."[14]

Unsurprisingly, virtue theory is congruent with what I present here, and in *Ecstatic Morality and Sexual Politics,* I showed how Thomas thinks of the virtues as ratifications of the core inclinations of natural law. Though it makes contemporary philosophers uncomfortable, Aristotle famously and provocatively invokes elements of natural law. Natural law is *law* and thus Hume's is/ought worry is misplaced. Max Scheler argued that the appeal of, and to, values avoids naturalism (values are in the "world" of the ought, so to say), but he also rejected the idea that morality was internally linked to obligation (against Hume and Kant, the "world" of the ought is not obligatory, not even for morals!).[15] I think Scheler is right that civilization is appealing in the same way that reprimitivism is aversive. Why Wojtyla wants to correct Scheler and reintroduce obligation into value theory is obvious.[16] Reprimitivism had (has?) massive appeal. The vitalism of National Socialism was in its avid embrace of reprimitivism, but embracing banality, as famously observed by Arendt, is as quick a route.

Here's a case in point. "Are new clothes a right, or a privilege? One of my friends (university educated and politically and culturally liberal) shops only at H&M. Her reasoning is she deserves to look good. But do we? Is access to new clothes a human right?"[17] It is a little hard to unpack the precise claim in "I deserve to look good." What could that argument be? The argument is more radical than saying "I want to look good, and my money gives really poor people a bit of money"—a sort of asymmetrical win-win proposal. I take it that the argument being made is also not that, because I am liberal and support all the right progressive causes, even really poor people should be happy to slave for me. That's just too absurd.

Since I am unsure of what is being claimed, let's settle on this: minimally, the speaker is claiming that she deserves to look good at the expense of the young girls who make a lot of H&M's clothes. The person refuses to spend money on clothes pricier than those at H&M, even though she knows that more costly clothes oftentimes reflect better working conditions. Somehow, she is owed, and they are not.

A theory of obligation is quick to correct this banality. Value theory is sometimes called intuitionism, and in Anglophone philosophy its most famous advocate is Sir W. D. Ross.[18] He identified seven prima facie duties, and this banality fails all seven. I will not go through them all, because I mention Ross now for other reasons. However, briefly, Ross observes that if you make a promise, then you have made a moral commitment to someone. Clearly, no young girls in Cambodia, or elsewhere, have made our ever-so-progressive fashionista a promise. They owe her no duty of fidelity. A second duty posits that, having done someone wrong, you owe them reparation: again, clearly, the young girls of Asia have done this woman no wrong. Indeed, the wrong runs in the other direction. Third, having received services, you owe a duty of gratitude. The relationship between our fashionista and the factory workers is not one of service but contract. The young girls in the factories owe no debt of gratitude. If we go down the list, it is clear our progressive is not owed anything, and her easy access to cheap, hip clothing has no anchor in obligation.

As I say, Ross discerns seven prima facie duties, and our banality case fails all of them. I mention Ross now, as intuitionism is in a period of revival after having been dismissed utterly for the last fifty years. Actually, Ross's theory is tremendously powerful, as you can use him to adjudicate case after case. A commentator wonders whether Ross fell out of fashion because of a worry that his theory commits someone to a weird ontological world of what R. L. Mackie called "queer facts."[19] To anyone reading Ross, it is quite evident his account of morals does not invoke any "queer facts," but mine certainly does: value tones.

Without any embarrassment, I invoke them. For authority, I am in good company: from Plato, to Shaftesbury and beyond, to the likes of Meinong. Phenomenology and child psychology give a warrant for this, as is clear from Reid, Scheler, and Merleau-Ponty. As Merleau-Ponty points out, flesh is baroque. Practices of marketing, branding, and design affirm value tones.[20] In the negative, so does ideology. Value confusion follows on metaphysical confusion, to invoke Przywara, and the historical studies I gave in this book show that bad metaphysics creates not merely moral problems but sometimes horror (reprimitivism). From another direction, Agamben argues we ignore value tones at our peril, but natural law and political theology show that value tones are an essential part of the span that puts distance between change and structure to prevent totalization. Totalitarianism has its origin in either univocity or equivocity but not in the deferred unity of the analogical spanning. This is what natural law as an expression of political theology secures.

Natural law is the remedy for modernity's failing humanism. The failure was inherited from the Middle Ages, and postmodernity has not found a way out. Humanism requires obedience to establishment—inclination lifted by liturgy—and to a hierarchy of value tones, which are themselves, at the last, "ultra things" of the veil of God. Natural law is the hope of Anselmian humanism and the Gregorian Reform, a *potentia obedientalis* lived out in games, dress-ups, and ritual. A legacy of the West, Thomism is proved to be as agile and soteriological as ever by Przywara.

NOTES

Preface

1. Erich Przywara, *Analogia Entis: Metaphysics; Original Structure and Universal Rhythm,* trans. John R. Betz and David Bentley Hart (Grand Rapids: Eerdmans, 2014).

2. Among a number of other places, the following discuss my account of natural law: John Milbank, "The New Divide," *Modern Theology* 26 (2010): 26–38, especially 37; Matt Levering, "Natural Law and Natural Inclinations: Rhonheimer, Pinckaers, McAleer," *Thomist* 70, no. 2 (April 2006): 155–201; Matt Levering, *Biblical Natural Law* (London: Oxford University Press, 2008), passim; Tracey Rowland, "Natural Law: From Neo-Thomism to Nuptial Mysticism," *Communio* 35 (Fall 2008): 376–96, especially 391–94; Tracey Rowland, *Catholic Theology* (London: Bloomsbury, 2017), 88; Fergus Kerr, *Twentieth-Century Catholic Theologians* (London: Blackwell, 2007), 181–84.

Introduction

1. "Faith, Reason and the University: Memories and Reflections" (lecture, University of Regensburg, Germany, September 12, 2006), https://w2.vatican.va/content/benedict-xvi/en/speeches/2006/september/documents/hf_ben-xvi_spe_20060912_university-regensburg.html.

2. Ruth Graham, "Just How Creepy Is 'Embryo Jewelry,' Exactly?" *Slate,* May 5, 2017, www.slate.com/blogs/xx_factor/2017/05/05/embryo_jewelry_is_creepy_but_how_creepy.html.

3. *Summa theologica* II-II, q. 100 (hereafter cited as *ST*).

4. See the following by the insightful Ian Bogost: "Why Nothing Works Anymore: Technology Has Its Own Purposes," *Atlantic,* February 23, 2017, www.theatlantic.com/technology/archive/2017/02/the-singularity-in-the-toilet-stall/517551/.

5. Levon Biss, "Sorry, Y'all—Humanity's Nearing an Upgrade to Irrelevance," *Wired,* February 21, 2017, www.wired.com/2017/02/yuval-harari-tech -is-the-new-religion/.

6. "AI Can Make Us All Dress Better: So Why Isn't the Fashion Industry Using It More?," *Fast Company,* February 25, 2017, www.fastcompany.com /3068172/robot-revolution/ai-can-make-us-all-dress-better-so-why-isnt-the -fashion-industry-using-it-m.

Chapter One

1. R. Martin, "Quelques 'premiers' maitres dominicains de Paris et d'Oxford et la soi-disant ecole dominicaine augustinienne" (1229–79), *Revue des sciences philosophiques et théologiques* 9 (1920): 580.

2. D. Callus, *The Condemnation of St. Thomas at Oxford* (Oxford: Blackfriars, 1955), 15. For others of the same opinion, see E. M. F. Sommer-Seckendorff, *Studies in the Life of Robert Kilwardby, O. P.* (Rome: Institutum Historicum FF. Praedicatorium, 1937), 145–46; G. Leff, *Paris and Oxford Universities in the Thirteenth and Fourteenth Centuries* (New York: John Wiley and Sons, 1968), 290–91; and A. Maurer, *Medieval Philosophy* (Toronto: Pontifical Institute of Medieval Studies, 1982), 206–7.

3. R. Schenk, "The Two Covenants in Medieval Theology," *Nova et Vetera: English Edition of the International Theological Journal* 4, no. 4 (Fall 2006): 894.

4. The thirty condemned propositions at Oxford are stated as condemned *de consensu omnium magistrorum Oxoniensium.* See Kilwardby, *Littera ad Petrum de Conflans,* ed. F. Ehrle, "Ein Schreiben des Erzbischofs von Canterbury Robert Kilwardby zur Rechtfertigung seiner Lehrverurtheilung vom 11. März 1277," *Archiv für Literatur und Kirchengeschichte des Mittelalters,* vol. 5 (1889): 614.

5. M. Chenu, "Robert Kilwardby," *Dictionnaire de théologie catholique,* vol. 8, pt. 2 (Paris: Letouzey et Ané, 1899–1950), 2, 355.

6. Cf. Albert Judy's introduction to R. Kilwardby, *De ortu scientiarum,* ed. A. Judy (Oxford: British Academy, 1976), xi.

7. The General Chapter of the Dominicans began an investigation, with impeachment power, of those defaming Thomas. See J. A. Weisheipl, "Sciences in the Thirteenth Century," in *The Early Oxford Schools,* ed. T. Henry Aston (Oxford: Oxford University Press, 1984), 467–68.

8. I owe the basic sense of this paragraph to private communications with Richard Schenk, OP. Father Schenk is a rich source of information about Robert, and I am happy to thank him here for his kindness.

9. For this common view, see R. Hissette, *Enquête sur les 219 articles condamnés a Paris le 7 mars 1277, Philosophes médiévaux,* vol. 22 (Louvian: Publications Universitaires, 1977); and J. Wippel, *The Metaphysical Thought of Godfrey of Fontaines: A Study in Late Thirteenth-Century Philosophy* (Washington, DC: Catholic University of America Press, 1981).

10. A point ably proven by Paul Thom. See his *Logic and Ontology in the Syllogistic of Robert Kilwardby* (Leiden: Brill, 2007).

11. P. Nemo, *What Is the West?* (Pittsburgh: Duquesne University Press, 2006).

12. H. Berman, *Law and Revolution* (Cambridge, MA: Harvard University Press, 1983).

13. To see Berman's point, think only of Aquinas's *De malo,* a commentary on Gregory's work on the deadly sins.

14. Nemo, *What Is the West?,* 44–49.

15. Nemo, *What Is the West?,* chap. 4.

16. M.-D. Chenu, *Les Réponses de S. Thomas et de Kilwardby a la consultation de Jean de Verceil* (1271), in *Mélanges Mandonnet,* vol. 1 (Paris: J. Vrin, 1930), q. 8, p. 200.

17. Chenu, *Les Réponses,* 213.

18. C. Schmitt, *Dictatorship* (Cambridge, MA: Polity, 2014), 34–35.

19. K. Barth, *Church Dogmatics,* ed. G. W. Bromiley and T. F. Torrance, trans. T. H. L. Parker, W. B. Johnston, Harold Knight, and J. L. M. Haire, vol. 2, pt. 1 (Edinburgh: T. and T. Clark, 1957), 211, and especially 239.

20. "I can see no third alternative between that exploitation of the *analogia entis* which is legitimate only on the basis of Roman Catholicism, between the greatness and misery of a so-called natural knowledge of God in the sense of the *Vaticanum,* and a Protestant theology which draws from its own source, which stands on its own feet, and which is finally liberated from this secular misery" (Barth, *Church Dogmatics,* xiii).

21. Chenu, "Robert Kilwardby," 2, 355; Martin, "Quelques 'premiers' maitres dominicains," 566.

22. See A. Robiglio, "Breaking the Great Chain of Being: A Note on the Paris Condemnations of 1277, Thomas Aquinas and the Proper Subject of Metaphysics," *Verbum* 6, no. 1 (2004): 51–59; and C. Normore, "Who Was Condemned in 1277?," *Modern Schoolman* 72 (1995): 273–81.

23. J. F. Silva, "Robert Kilwardby," in *The Stanford Encyclopedia of Philosophy,* ed. Edward N. Zalta (Fall 2014), http://plato.stanford.edu/archives/fall2014/entries/robert-kilwardby/.

24. See his *Itinerarium,* chap. 2. Such a treatment finds an echo in an unlikely place: Schopenhauer.

25. Please see my "The Science of Music: A Platonic Application of the *Posterior Analytics* in Robert Kilwardby's *De ortu scientiarum*," *Acta Philosophica* 12 (2003): 323–35.

26. See E. Peterson, "The Book on the Angels: Their Place and Meaning in the Liturgy," in *Theological Tractates,* ed. M. J. Hollerich (Stanford, 2011), 106–42. An example from the twentieth century is found in the magnificent opening pages of Tolkien's *Silmarillion.*

27. Indeed, when speaking of the world's *consonantia,* Thomas subscribes to the position of Dionysius, who thinks of sound not as song but as God's voice summoning all things: "secundum ordinem creaturam ad Deum et hanc tangit cum dicit quod Deus est causa consonantiae, sicut vocans omnia ad seipsum" (Thomas's commentary on Dionysius's *Divine Names,* as quoted by Brendan Sammon in his interesting *The God Who Is Beauty* [Eugene, OR: Pickwick, 2013], 305; according to the order of creatures to God, and this holds when he says that God is the cause of harmony, just as God calling all things to himself).

28. Some Catholic intellectuals think that Augustine and Thomas are really rather close intellectually. See the collection of essays in *Aquinas the Augustinian,* ed. M. Dauphinais, M. Levering, and B. David (Washington, DC: Catholic University of America Press, 2007). Przywara argues otherwise. For my sense of some acute differences between Thomas and Augustine, especially as brought to the fore in early fourteenth-century philosophy, see my essay "Pleasure: A Reflection on Benedict XVI's *Deus Caritas Est,*" *Nova et Vetera: English Edition of the International Theological Journal* 5, no. 2 (2007): 315–24.

29. J. F. Silva and J. Toivanen, "The Active Nature of the Soul in Sense Perception: Robert Kilwardby and Peter John Olivi," *Vivarium* 48 (2010): 245–78.

30. "Pulchritdo enim est numerosa aequalitas secundum Augustinum in 6 *Musicae*" (F. Stegmüller, "Der Traktat des Robert Kilwardby, 'De imagine et vestigio Trinitatis'," *Archives d'histoire doctrinal et littéraire du moyen âge* 10–11 [1935–36]: 357). "Alia enim causa [multiplicationis individuorum] est perfectio universi in decore, quae per numerositatem magis habetur, quia, ut dicit Augustinus in VI Musicae, pulchritudo est numerosa aequalitas" (R. Kilwardby, *Quaestiones in lib. II Sententiarum,* ed. G. Leibold [Munich: Bayerische Akademie der Wissenschaften, 1992], q. 20, ll. 25–27, p. 79; the other cause of the multiplicity of individuals is the perfection of the universe in adornment, which is better had by great number, because, as Augustine says in part six of his *de Musica,* beauty is numbered symmetry). Text references are to this edition.

31. Unsurprisingly, therefore, Robert subscribes to Augustine's position that faith is lodged in an affective power, not an intellectual one, as most Dominicans

held (L.-B. Gillon, "Structure et genèse de la foi, d'après Robert Kilwardby," *Revue Thomiste* [1955]: 629–36).

32. Giles of Rome makes the same argument. See my "Disputing the Unity of the World: The Importance of *res* and the Influence of Averroes in Giles of Rome's Critique of Thomas Aquinas over the Unity of the World," *Journal of the History of Philosophy* 36, no. 1 (1998): 29–55.

33. Please see my "Matter and the Unity of Being in the Philosophical Theology of Saint Thomas Aquinas," *Thomist* 61, no. 2 (1997): 257–77.

34. R. Kilwardby, *Quaestiones in lib. II Sententiarum*, ed. G. Leibold (Munich: Bayerische Akademie der Wissenschaften, 1992), q. 17, l. 143, p. 65 (hereafter cited as II *Sent.*). Cf. F. Stegmüller, "Der Traktat des Robert Kilwardby, O. P., 'De imagine et vestigio Trinitatis'"; R. Kilwardby, *De natura relationis*, ed. L. Schmücker (Brixen, Südtirol: A. Weger, 1980).

35. Please see my "The Presence of Averroes in the Natural Philosophy of Robert Kilwardby," *Archiv für Geschichte der Philosophie* 81 (1999): 33–54.

36. II *Sent.* q. 85, ll. 46–51, p. 239; cf. "Ergo ille per calorem, et calor per spiritum, distinguit partes in semine et distinctas effigiat antequam cibetur educens *de potentia intima concepti* vegetativam, per quam nutriatur et augeatur. Effigiando vero partes, simul disponit ad sensum, producens partite potentiam sensitivam, et exit ista de interioribus materia prius disposite per vegetativam. Et hec forma sensitiva . . . ultima est et potissima in operibus omnibus que de elementis et elementatis produci possit" (Chenu, *Les Réponses*, 208, emphasis added; Therefore, through heat, and heat through spirit, it distinguishes and fashions distinct parts in the seed before it is fed, drawing the vegetative soul from the inner power of the conceptum, by which the conceptum is nourished and grows. In fashioning the parts of the vegetative soul, it readies for sensation at the same time, producing with proper divisions the sensitive power; it becomes that power from interior parts, the matter having been properly prepared by the action of the vegetative soul. The sensitive form is the highest possibility from the elements and what can be made from them.). For other citations, please see my "Presence of Averroes," especially 43.

37. Please see my "Was Medical Theory Heterodox in the Latin Middle Ages? The Plurality Theses of Paul of Venice and the Medical Authorities, Galen, Haly Abbas and Averroes," *Recherches de Theologie et Philosophie Medievales* 68 (2001): 349–70.

38. R. Kilwardby, *Quaestiones in lib. III Sententiarum*, ed. E. Gossmann (Munich: Bayerische Akademie der Wissenschaften, 1982), q. 47, ll. 111–16, p. 221 (hereafter cited as III *Sent.*). Cf. Kilwardby, *Littera ad Petrum*, 622–23.

39. III *Sent.* q. 46, ll. 620–23, p. 215.

40. Cf. Karl Rahner, "Current Problems in Christology," *Theological Investigations*, vol. 1 (Baltimore: Helicon Press, 1965), 149–200.

41. "Patet igitur quid hic intelligendum per naturam, scilicet individuam naturam in genere humano, et quid per personam, scilicet res in actu sui generis, manens distincte ab omnibus aliis" (III *Sent.* q. 8, ll. 123–25, p. 40).

42. "Similiter, si sit principium materiale alicuius rei quae iam in actu sit vel esse possit, non est in actu completo sui generis, et ideo proprie nullum horum est individuum vel persona sed tantum aliquo modo singular" (III *Sent.* q. 8, ll. 105–7, p. 39; similarly, if there is a material principle of such a thing which already is or could be in act, it is not in the complete act of its genus, and so properly nothing of this sort is an individual or a person only a singular in some manner).

43. "Nec est hoc inconveniens quod idem individuet et individuetur, signet et signetur a se secundum diversas rationes. Inquantum enim forma continet materiam, indistanter individuat et signat. Inquantum autem materiae indistanter unitae adhaeret, individuatur et signatur" (II *Sent.* q. 17, ll. 109–112, p. 64; It is not unsuitable that the same thing individuates and is individuated, is marked and puts a mark upon itself, according to different grounds. Insofar as form contains matter, it distinguishes and individuates without separation. Insofar as form adheres without separation to matter, it is marked out and individuated.).

44. "Sicut persona puri hominis habet suum esse ex compositione corporis et animae. . . . Sed nunc aliter est, quia persona Christi habet suum esse a Patre ab aeterno, absque omni unione cum humana natura, et humana natura adveniens nihil ei confert personalitatis, sed ad ea suscipit personalitatem" (III *Sent.* q. 14, ll. 44–48, p. 68; Just as the personhood of a regular human has its being from the composition of body and soul. . . . But in this case it is otherwise, because the person of Christ has his being eternally from the father, without any union-to-human nature, and human nature coming confers nothing on his personhood but rather defers to Christ's personhood.).

45. "Persona puri hominis est res eiusdem generis, quia est id ipsum quod natura, sed secundum aliam rationem, et ideo sicut natura composita, sic et persona. Sed persona Christi non est res alterius generis quam divina natura, et ideo quamvis uniatur ei humana natura, quae est res alterius generis et personetur per illam, non sequitur quod persona sit composita, et ut breviter dicam, persona puri hominis est idem cum natura composita, persona Christi est idem cum natura simplicissima. Ideo illa semper composita est, sed haec simplex" (III *Sent.* q. 14, ll. 49–55, p. 68; The personhood of a regular human is a thing in its own genus, because it is itself a nature, albeit according to another ground, and so just as a composed nature, so personhood. But the person of Christ is not a thing of another genus than the divine nature, yet although human nature is

united to the person of Christ, which is a thing of another genus and is made into a person through Christ, it does not follow that that person is a composite, so in short I say, a regular human's personhood is the same as its composed nature, the person of Christ is the same as God's most simple nature. So the human person is always a composite, but the divine simple.).

46. It is noteworthy that when discussing Thomas on the Incarnation, Przywara latches onto a late work by Thomas, *De unione Verbi incarnati*. This text is notorious among Thomists, for its account of Christ's *esse* is significantly different from elsewhere in Thomas. Most commentators are stumped by the divergence. For an excellent assessment of the problems raised by *De unione*, see V. Salas, "Thomas Aquinas on Christ's *Esse*: The Metaphysics of the Incarnation," *Thomist* 70 (2006): 577–603. Przywara sees *De unione* as a culmination of Thomas's insight into the *analogia entis*. He is less anxious about *De unione* because, unlike contemporary commentators, he begins with Thomas's claim in *De Veritate* that God is more intimate to the creature than it is to itself. The Incarnation is an intensification of this intimacy: as Przywara puts it, "a radically positive unity is declared" (*AE*, 305). In my opinion, Przywara is playing with something like the difference between natural and divine positive law. The Incarnation is no change in natural order but an exuberant articulation of a latent possibility that shifts our vision from the natural to the sacral universe (*AE*, 306). As is the case with an anamorphic painting or object, the sacral universe has always been the structural reality, but a pivot in cognition is necessary to reveal it within the natural. See Lacan's pages on the anamorphic for this point, in *The Seminar of Jacques Lacan Book VII: The Ethics of Psychoanalysis 1959–1960* (New York: Norton, 1992), chaps. 10 and 11.

Chapter Two

1. This chapter relies, in part, on my "1277 and the Causality of Damnation in Giles of Rome," *Modern Schoolman* 83 (May 2006): 285–300.

2. The propositions and their exact wording are listed in many places, but see F.-X. Putallaz, "L'âme et le feu: Notes franciscaines sur le feu de l'enfer après 1277," in *Nach der verurteilung von 1277: Philosophie und Theologie an der Universität von Paris im letzten Viertel des 13. Jahrhunderts: Studien und Texte*, ed. J. A. Aertsen, K. Emery, and A. Speer (Berlin: W. de Gruyter, 2001), 889–901.

3. For a brilliant contemporary treatment of these questions, see B. O'Shaughnessy, *The Will*, vol. 1 (Cambridge: Cambridge University Press, 1983).

4. G. Agamben, *The Highest Poverty* (Stanford, CA: Stanford University Press, 2013).

5. Bible citations are from the King James version.

6. P. J. Olivi, *Quaestiones de novissimis ex summa super IV sententiarum*, ed. P. Maranesi (Rome: Editiones Collegii S. Bonaventurae, 2004), pt. 4, q. 7, ll. 35–40, p. 150 (hereafter cited as *QN*).

7. See J. Capreolus, *Defensiones Theologiae Divi Thomae Aquinatis*, eds. C. Paban and T. Pégues, 7 vols. (Turin: Alfred Cattier, 1900–1908), bk. 4, d. 44, q. 4, p. 98. Please see my "Duns Scotus and Giles of Rome on Whether Sensations Are Intentional," in *John Duns Scotus, Philosopher, Archa Verbi 3*, ed. M. B. Ingham (Münster: Aschendorff Verlag, 2010), 111–18.

8. "Quod in animabus damnatis et daemonibus intellectus fungitur vice sensus: et quod tales substantiae cremantur, quia vident, id est, sentiunt se cremari" (A. Romanus, *De predestinatione et prescientia, de paradiso et inferno, et ubi predestinati et presciti sunt finaliter Collocandi*, chap. 13).

9. Romanus, *De predestinatione,* chap. 13, p. 42rbd.

10. Putallaz, "L'âme et le feu," 892–94.

11. Sylvain Piron, "The Formation of Olivi's Intellectual Project," *Oliviana* 1 (2003).

12. As to Giles's Augustinian pedigree, please see my articles on the role Augustine plays, respectively, in his anthropology, political theory, and conception of the brittleness of the created order: "Sensuality: An Avenue into the Political and Metaphysical Thought of Giles of Rome," *Gregorianum* 82 (2001): 129–47; "Giles of Rome on Political Authority," *Journal of the History of Ideas* 60 (1999): 21–36; "Disputing the Unity of the World: The Importance of *Res* and the Influence of Averroes in Giles of Rome's Critique of Thomas Aquinas over the Unity of the World," *Journal of the History of Philosophy* 36 (1998): 29–55.

13. N. Malebranche, *The Search after Truth* (Cambridge: Cambridge University Press, 1997), 3.

14. S. Nadler "Malebranche on Causation," in *The Cambridge Companion to Malebranche,* ed. S. Nadler (Cambridge: Cambridge University Press, 2000), 114; cf. A. Pyle, *Malebranche* (London: Routledge, 2003), 98.

15. "Anima autem solum immutatur intentionaliter, quia solum sentit, sive (ut proprie dicatur) percipit laesionem et dolet et cruciatur maxime" (Romanus, *De predestinatione,* chap. 12, p. 42vba; Only the soul changes intentionally, because only it feels, or [more properly speaking] perceives the wound and greatly suffers and is tormented); "Nam percipere se dolere est dolere: qui autem dolorem non percipit nequaquam dolet" (A. Romanus, *Quodlibet II, Quodlibeta* [Frankfurt: Minerva, 1966], q. 3, p. 72b; For to perceive oneself to suffer, is to suffer: one who does not perceive the pain in no way suffers).

16. "Nam licet in inferno esset anima divitis non habentis corporalem lin-guam, tamen talis cruciatus virtute Dei poterat causari in anima separata per intellectum, qualis fieri poterat eo vivente, per linguam, et sensum" (A. Roma-nus, *De predestinatione,* chap. 13, p. 43rbc; Although the rich man's soul in hell would not have a physical tongue, torment of such a kind is able to be caused by God in a separated soul through the mind, just like when living through the tongue and sense); cf. Capreolus, *Defensiones Theologiae,* bk. 4, d. 44, q. 4, p. 113, col. a.

17. Romanus, *De predestinatione,* chap. 12, p.42vba; cf. Romanus, *Quodli-bet II, Quodlibeta,* q. 3, p. 73a.

18. M. Scheler, *Formalism in Ethics and Nonformal Ethics of Values* (Evan-ston, IL: Northwestern University Press, 1973), 58.

19. Capreolus, *Defensiones Theologiae,* bk. 4, d. 44, q. 4, p. 114, col. a.

20. Capreolus, *Defensiones Theologiae,* bk. 4, d. 44, q. 4, p. 114, col. a.

21. Romanus, *De predestinatione,* chap. 12, p. 43rad; cf. A. Romanus, *Repor-tatio lecturae super Libras I–IV sententiarum,* ed. C. Luna, *Aegidii Romani Opera Omnia,* vol. 3.2 (Florence: Edizioni del Galluzzo, 2003), 480.

22. A. Kolnai, *Disgust* (Chicago: Open Court, 2004).

23. R. Ingarden, *Ontology of the Work of Art* (Athens: Ohio University Press, 1989), 318.

24. What follows is a modified version of my "1277 and the Sensations of the Damned: Peter John Olivi and the Augustinian Origins of Early Modern Angelism," *Studia Patristica* 87 (2015): 59–66.

25. This theory reappears centuries later in Lacan. What Lacan calls "the to-pology of the subject" plays the role of a sieve leading to "a deep subjectivisation of the outside world" (*The Seminar of Jacques Lacan Book VII: The Ethics of Psy-choanalysis 1959–1960* [New York: W. W. Norton, 1992], 46–51).

26. Cf. L. Spruit, *Species Intelligibilis: From Perception to Knowledge,* vol. 1 (Leiden: Brill, 1994), 216, 220.

27. P. J. Olivi, "Quaestio de locutionibus angelorum," *Oliviana* (December 31, 2003), c. 7, q. 7–8, para. 34, http://oliviana.revues.org/18.

28. "Est enim in substantiis spiritualibus duplex motus et ad presens unus est quo tota eorum substantia de uno loco vadit ad alium locum, alius est quo acies et virtuales aspectus seu intenciones suarum potentiarum hac vel illac ad diversa obiecta prohiciuntur seu diriguntur, sicut experimur in nobis, non solum quando ad varia cogitanda vel videnda movemur, sed etiam quando in inicio ingressus in sompnum sentimus intenciones sensuum interiorum et exteriorum retrahi ad interior, in hora vero excitacionis sentimus eas virtualiter protrahi ad exterior. Et hoc ipsum docet Augustinus tam XII *Super Genesim ad litteram* quam in libro *De Trinitate*" (Olivi, "Quaestio de locutionibus angelorum" para. 17).

Chapter Three

1. A. Schopenhauer, *The World as Will and Representation*, 2 vols., trans. E. F. J. Payne (New York: Dover, 1969), 1:99 (hereafter cited as *WWR*, followed by volume and page number).

2. This chapter is a heavily modified version of my essay "Who Gets the Best of the Winged Cherub? Reid and Schopenhauer Confront Early Modern Angelism," in *Schopenhauer's Fourfold Root*, ed. J. Head and D. Vanden Auweele, 115–25 (New York: Routledge, 2017). This article contains a lot more detail about Schopenhauer's theory of sensation.

3. T. Reid, *Inquiry and Essays* (Indianapolis: Hackett, 1983), 40, 44 (hereafter cited as *IE*). Cf. Thomas Reid, *Thomas Reid's Lectures on the Fine Arts* (The Hague: Nijhoff, 1973), 22–23.

4. For the medieval background to Berkeley's angelism, see C. S. Peirce, "Fraser's Edition of the Works of George Berkeley," in *Collected Papers of Charles Sanders Peirce*, ed. C. Hartshorne, P. Weiss, and A. Burks, vol. 8 (Cambridge, MA: Harvard University Press, 1958), 9–38.

5. R. Descartes, *Meditations and Other Metaphysical Writings* (London: Penguin, 2003). There are, of course, a number of passages like this.

6. Contrasting him with such "a thoroughly contemptible fellow as Hegel," Schopenhauer compliments Reid for his "excellent book" *Inquiry into the Human Mind* and cites the first edition of 1764 and the sixth edition of 1810. The book is "very instructive and well worth reading," because it offers a "thorough and acute demonstration that the collective sensations of the senses do not bear the least resemblance to the world known through perception" (A. Schopenhauer, *On the Fourfold Root of the Principle of Sufficient Reason*, trans. D. E. Cartwright, E. E. Erdmann, and C. Janaway [Cambridge: Cambridge University Press, 2012], 16 [hereafter cited as *FR*]). This position is "very clearly and beautifully described by Dr. Thomas Reid" (*WWR*, 2:191).

7. "The intellect is really like the reflecting surface of water, but the water itself is like the will, whose disturbance therefore at once destroys the clearness of that mirror and the distinctness of its images" (*WWR*, 2:430).

8. "Without this intellectual operation [application of the law of causality], for which the forms must lie ready in us, the perception of an *objective, external world* could never arise from a mere *sensation* within our skin" (*WWR*, 2:208).

9. R. Descartes, *Meditations and Other Metaphysical Writings* (New York: Penguin, 2003), 28–29.

10. G. Berkeley, *Three Dialogues between Hylas and Philonous* (Oxford: Oxford University Press, 2003), 127; see also 113, 129–30.

11. Merleau-Ponty finds confirmation of this point among twentieth-century scientists in *The Visible and the Invisible* (Evanston, IL: Northwestern University Press, 1968), 16–18.

12. "That those things do really exist which we distinctly perceive by our senses, and are what we perceive them to be" (*IE,* 278); cf. Reid, *Thomas Reid's Lectures,* 39.

13. In *The Visible and the Invisible,* Merleau-Ponty expresses this idea: "language is not a mask over Being, but—if one knows how to grasp it with all its roots and all its foliation—the most valuable witness to Being."

14. For Reid's reliance on models of evidence in use in the Scottish courts of his time, see W. Davis, *Thomas Reid's Ethics: Moral Epistemology on Legal Foundations* (New York: Bloomsbury, 2006), especially chapter 3 on witness procedure in Scottish law.

15. O. Sacks, "To See and Not See," in *An Anthropologist on Mars* (New York: Knopf, 1995), 143.

16. Sacks, "To See," 123.

17. Sacks, "To See," 123.

18. Sacks, "To See," 117.

19. Cf. *Thomas Reid's Lectures,* 49.

20. Patrick Gardiner raises some similar worries with Schopenhauer's account. See P. Gardiner, *Schopenhauer* (New York: Penguin, 1962), 106–9.

21. Gardiner, *Schopenhauer,* 19.

Chapter Four

1. *The World as Will and Representation,* 2 vols., trans. E. F. J. Payne (New York: Dover, 1969), 1:203 (hereafter cited as *WWR*).

2. An earlier, and very different, version of this chapter exists in English and German. However, in the chapter here, I have done a much better job of applying Przywara's logic to Nazism. For my earlier attempts, see "Nazi Sexual Politics: Aurel Kolnai on the Threat of Re-primitivism," in *Aurel Kolnai's* The War against the West *Reconsidered* (New York: Routledge, 2019); and "Sexualpolitik des Nationalsozialismus: Aurel Kolnai zur Gefahr eines Rückfalls in den Primitivismus," in Aurel Kolnais, *Der Krieg gegen den Westen: Eine Debatte,* ed. Wolfgang Bialas (Göttingen: Vandenhoeck and Ruprecht, 2018), 185–97.

3. A. Kolnai, *The War against the West* (London: Victor Gollancz, 1938) (hereafter cited as *WAW*). Though living in Austria at the time, Kolnai wrote the book in English. Under the auspices of the Hannah Arendt Institute, with

funding from the German government, Wolfgang Bialas, a German scholar of the Nazi period, took four years to translate this hefty book into German, chasing down all the sources Kolnai used. See Aurel Kolnai, *Der Krieg gegen den Westen,* ed. Wolfgang Bialas (Göttingen: Vandenhoeck and Ruprecht, 2015). I also rely on essays in A. Kolnai, *Politics, Values, and National Socialism* (London: Transaction, 2013) (hereafter cited as *PVNS*).

4. E. Burke, *Reflections on the Revolution in France* (Indianapolis: Liberty Fund, 1999), 180.

5. For an interesting contemporary debate about this, see A. Pidel, "Erich Przywara, S.J., and 'Catholic Fascism,'" *Journal for the History of Modern Theology* 23, no. 1 (2016): 27–55.

6. A. Kolnai, "Privilege and Liberty," in *Privilege and Liberty and Other Essays in Political Philosophy* (Lanham, MD: Lexington Books, 1999).

7. Kolnai, "Privilege and Liberty," 108. I discuss Kolnai's observations about the totalitarian aspirations internal to humanitarianism in *Ecstatic Morality and Sexual Politics* (New York: Fordham University Press, 2005).

8. Kolnai, "Privilege and Liberty," 105.

9. Kolnai, "Privilege and Liberty," 106.

10. Kolnai, "Privilege and Liberty," 106.

11. A. Kolnai, "The Sovereignty of the Object," in *Ethics, Value, and Reality* (London: Transaction Press, 2008).

12. Kolnai, "Sovereignty of the Object," 210–13.

13. Kolnai, "Sovereignty of the Object," 318.

14. Burke, *Reflections on the Revolution,* 122.

15. Kolnai, "Privilege and Liberty," 111.

16. *Ethics, Value, and Reality* (London: Transaction, 2017), 165–85.

17. G. Agamben, *The Highest Poverty* (Stanford, CA: Stanford University Press, 2011), xiii, 144–45.

18. Agamben, *Highest Poverty,* 86–87.

Chapter Five

1. G. Agamben, *The Highest Poverty* (Stanford, CA: Stanford University Press, 2011), xiii.

2. C. Schmitt, *Political Theology* (Chicago: University of Chicago Press, 2005), 46.

3. G. Agamben, *The Kingdom and the Glory* (Stanford, CA: Stanford University Press, 2011), 158 (hereafter cited as *KG*).

4. C. Schmitt, *Dictatorship* (Cambridge: Polity, 2014), 83.

5. G. Agamben, *Stasis: Civil War as a Political Paradigm* (Stanford, CA: Stanford, 2015), 47–49; cf. Schmitt, *Dictatorship*, 83.

6. Agamben, *Highest Poverty,* 144.

7. D. G. Leahy, *Foundation: Matter the Body Itself* (Albany: SUNY Press, 1996), 579 (hereafter cited as *Foundation*).

8. D. G. Leahy, *Beyond Sovereignty: A New Global Ethics and Morality* (Aurora, CO: Davies Group, 2010), 185 (hereafter cited as *Beyond*).

9. Agamben, *Highest Poverty,* 144–45.

10. J. Courtney Murray, *We Hold These Truths* (New York: Sheed and Ward, 1960), 298.

11. That is, the idea of action emergent from changes in the Western conception of action and primarily derived from Catholic theology. Agamben terms this idea of action *operativity,* playing on sacramental causality and the phrase *ex opera operato.* The reality of our action is sacramental, and just as the priest in fact completes a work in his body by the action of Christ, so we (now secularized) complete works in our bodies by the action of the state and capital. See G. Agamben, *Opus Dei: An Archaeology of Duty* (Stanford, CA: Stanford University Press, 2013), 22–23.

12. Please see my discussion in the introduction to *Veneration & Refinement: The Ethics of Fashion,* online publication, *ethicsoffashion.com.*

13. In a footnote, Leahy directs readers to passages where he discusses clothes, or the "body itself as clothing itself" (*Beyond,* 241n49). He cites *Foundation,* 559ff., 578ff., 592ff.

14. See Adam Smith's fascinating account of a man growing up alone on a desert island, in *Theory of Moral Sentiments* (Carmel, IN: Liberty Fund, 1976), 110–11.

15. Editing this book coincided with a find of early humans dating to about three hundred thousand years ago. Minimally, we can say clothing and decoration are very old, and I am not aware of any record of utterly unadorned human peoples. This point is also made by Jacques Lacan in his comments on the vase and the "fabricated signifier." See *The Seminar of Jacques Lacan Book VII: The Ethics of Psychoanalysis 1959–1960* (New York: Norton, 1992), 120–22.

16. Someone might think that clothing itself is a surrogate for angelism, but I think clothing as an embossing gets at the important point that contours of body and self are shown in clothing. It is noticeable that Lacan always speaks of the Thing—in relationship to which the subject exists—as veiled, and not as behind a mask or a curtain (*Seminar of Jacques Lacan,* 118). A veil could approximate a curtain, if it were heavy enough, and thus obscure the lines of the face utterly, but oftentimes a veil is a witness to what is behind. For this very point,

see M. Merleau-Ponty, *The Visible and the Invisible* (Evanston, IL: Northwestern University Press, 1968), 126.

17. Agamben is keen to stress the role of the Augustinian priest and seminal Early Modern philosopher Malebranche in Smith's thinking (*KG,* 283–84).

18. Cf. Lacan, *Seminar of Jacques Lacan,* 89.

19. On this point, see Max Scheler's criticism of Thomas, in *The Nature of Sympathy* (New York: Routledge, 2008), 121. It's the same charge Kilwardby levels.

20. *Theory of Moral Sentiments,* 50.

21. M. Bakunin, *Statism and Anarchy* (Cambridge: Cambridge University Press, 2005), 133–35.

22. Agamben, *Highest Poverty,* 144, 134–35.

23. Agamben, *Highest Poverty,* 125.

24. Agamben, *Highest Poverty,* 136.

Chapter Six

1. M. Merleau-Ponty, *The Visible and the Invisible* (Evanston, IL: Northwestern University Press, 1968) (hereafter cited as *VI*).

2. Bakunin, *Statism and Anarchy,* 155, 133–35, among many pages.

3. M. Merleau-Ponty, *Signs* (Evansville, IL: Northwestern University Press, 1972), 167.

4. Merleau-Ponty, *Signs,* 181.

5. E. Alloa, *Resistance of the Sensible World* (New York: Fordham University Press, 2017), 80–81.

6. An extremely interesting 1960 note on the embryo runs, "When the embryo's organism starts to perceive . . . the vortex of the embryogenesis suddenly centers itself upon the interior hollow it was preparing—A certain fundamental divergence, a certain constitutive dissonance emerges—The mystery is the same as that by which a child slides into language" (*VI,* 233–34). If we follow the image of the hollow or the furrow, then the invisible, the idea or the object of consciousness, which is also the visible in its other (material) aspect, happens inside the space of the vacuole. The hollow reminds one of Lacan's vase, an image he gives for the Thing. But the reference to embryology also puts one in mind of Lacan's talk of the Thing—a fraught gap in our basic experience—as a vacuole. In Lacan, the Thing is the place of a union desired, but unattained: the site is open, therefore, and perpetually so (castration). The Thing marks the fecund site of estrangement (from the mother, or feminine object). For Lacan, persons are creative, because they are wounded. Lacan does

not use the image of the vacuole much—he says it was suggested to him by a seminar member—but it is highly suggestive. An image of fecundity, the vacuole gives body to a cell and manages what is troublesome, absorbing and expelling alien bacteria or waste. Our psyche orbits around an *amor interruptus*, as Lacan casts the vacuole. It generates desire but also deflects its satisfaction: "There are also detours and obstacles which are organized so as to make the domain of the vacuole stand out as such. What gets to be projected as such is a certain transgression of desire." See J. Lacan, *The Seminar of Jacques Lacan Book VII: The Ethics of Psychoanalysis 1959–1960* (New York: W. W. Norton, 1992), 150–52.

7. *At the very least*, intimates: Merleau-Ponty likes the idea of polymorphism because he does not want to think of objects or values as discrete essences (*VI*, 206–7); cf. M. Merleau-Ponty, *The Primacy of Perception* (Evanston, IL: Northwestern University Press, 1982), 5. The red dress is red by "com-position," that is, it is only what it is by its relationship with other reds about it and even other colors: this is why being is said to be a texture (*VI*, 207). I think Shaftesbury's account of value tones is compatible with this polymorphism. In pointillism, the tones still come to visibility: Merleau-Ponty speaks of "the grain of the colour." I also think a "hard" doctrine of value tones is possible. Proust, an important test case for Merleau-Ponty, tends this way, as does Merleau-Ponty himself at times (*VI*, 205, 209).

8. Merleau-Ponty uses this phrase a number of times. It refers to indistinct objects in the world of children—objects that populate the horizon of their world but that escape their complete conceptual grasp. Though Merleau-Ponty does not say this, I think that implicit in his idea of flesh is a claim that metaphysically we are all comparable to children in this regard (*Primacy of Perception*, 99), albeit to different degrees.

9. A. A. Cooper, *Characteristics of Men, Manners, Opinions, Times* (Cambridge: Cambridge University Press, 2012), 416–17.

10. Merleau-Ponty, *Signs*, 174.

11. It is a little unclear how liquid Merleau-Ponty thought this "vaginal" potency was. As noted in note 6 of this chapter, there are places where he speaks of "hard" value tones. If it is too liquid, he will loose the bow to the sovereignty of the object, but of course his Leftism might welcome the transformational and revolutionary possibilities of a lack of deference. The problem here, though, is whether he would have slipped back into Cartesianism, a univocity of omnipotent divine will. And if he had, an added worry would be that his philosophy is not phenomenological but ideological.

12. Merleau-Ponty, *Signs*, 165, 181.

13. Cooper, *Characteristics of Men*, 351–52; cf. 172–73.

14. Reid, *Thomas Reid's Lectures*, 39, 47.

15. H. Samuel, "France Says Marks and Spencer Burkini 'Irresponsible,'" *Telegraph,* March 30, 2016, www.telegraph.co.uk/news/2016/03/30/france-says -marks-and-spencer-burkini-irresponsible/.

16. C. Bohlen, "The Multifaceted 'Burkini' Debate," *New York Times,* August 23, 2016, www.nytimes.com/2016/08/23/world/europe/france-veil-burkini-hijab .html?_r=0.

17. M. Cyrus, "We Can't Stop," official video, June 19, 2013, www.youtube .com/watch?v=LrUvu1mlWco.

18. Samuel, "Marks and Spencer Burkini."

19. E. Burke, *Reflections on the Revolution in France,* vol. 2 of *Select Works of Edmund Burke* (Carmel, IN: Liberty Fund, 1999), 119.

20. Merleau-Ponty, *Primacy of Perception,* 6.

21. See also Merleau-Ponty, *Primacy of Perception,* 4, 18.

Chapter Seven

1. C. Lefort, *Democracy and Political Theory* (Cambridge: Polity Press, 1988), 20, 233. Agamben makes the same claim in *The Highest Poverty* (9, 83).

2. See essays 7 and 8 in *Politics, Values, and National Socialism.*

3. *Ecstatic Morality and Sexual Politics: A Catholic and Antitotalitarian View of the Body* (New York: Fordham University Press, 2005). If I may be permitted to reply to some critics, both Marika Rose and Gerard Loughlin make the claim that my focus on the wound of love means I cannot defend my claim that Christianity is built on a metaphysics of peace (see M. Rose, "The Body and Ethics in Thomas Aquinas's *Summa Theologiae,*" *New Blackfriars* 96 [2013]: 540–51). As I point out in a number of places in the book—when I speak about nature and grace and original sin, as well as when I discuss Levinas—the metaphysics of the body means that the body is inevitably morally fraught, but the body is also at its origin generous (ecstatic). The body is double in aspect, tending to self-absorption *and* to generosity: the inclinations of natural law thus wound *the other* propensity of the body to self-concern. Of course, this metaphysical problem is compounded by historical accretions of disorder. My body—its genetic history, national and economic habitus, and personal habits—means generosity cannot but wound my proclivities even more. For a more careful reading, please see N. Zimmermann, *Facing the Other* (Eugene, OR: Cascade, 2015), 185–86.

4. Much of what follows is a highly modified version of a response I delivered to Leon Kass's work on the Ten Commandments. Professor Kass was being honored by the Father Ernest Fortin Foundation, and I was asked to deliver a

response to Kass's reflections. Leon Kass is a leading American intellectual and the author of many books, including his important *Towards a More Natural Science*. Professor Kass is also a generous-spirited man. I am highly indebted to his work on the Ten Commandments in what follows. He helped me think through the problem of idolatry. Professor Kass's essay is part of a work in progress, so I have deleted quotations. However, here he is at Harvard University talking about the topic at length: Leon Kass, "The Ten Commandments" (lecture, Program on Constitutional Government, Harvard University, Cambridge, MA, June 29, 2016), video, 1:32, www.youtube.com/watch?v=WBfCSXA8jR0.

5. *Veritatis Splendor,* encyclical (1993), para. 79, with reference to *ST* I–II, q. 100, a. 1 http://w2.vatican.va/content/john-paul-ii/en/encyclicals/documents /hf_jp-ii_enc_06081993_veritatis-splendor.html (hereafter cited as *VS*).

6. For non-American readers, the Second Amendment is one of the founding documents of American life. Ratified in 1791, it permits widespread gun ownership in the United States. It has become politically controversial in recent years.

7. Cf. F. de Vitoria, *Political Writings* (Cambridge: Cambridge University Press, 2001), 160.

8. De Vitoria, *Political Writings,* 173.

9. Personal communication, March 16, 2017.

10. De Vitoria, *Political Writings,* 189.

11. Cf. de Vitoria, *Political Writings,* 171.

12. W. D. Ross affirms the Thomistic point, listing gratitude among the benefits received as one of seven prima facie moral duties. See *The Right and the Good* (Oxford: Oxford University Press, 2002), 21. Perhaps it also grounds the duty to bury the dead?

13. M. Bain, "A Designer Will Grow Alexander McQueen's Skin in a Lab to Use for Leather Bags and Jackets, *Quartz,* July 16, 2016, http://qz.com/731893 /a-designer-will-grow-alexander-mcqueens-skin-in-a-lab-to-use-for-leather-bags -and-jackets/.

14. "The Macabre World of Books Bound in Human Skin, *BBC News* on-line, June 20, 2014, www.bbc.com/news/magazine-27903742.

15. "World Fame of Worcester Cathedral Library, June 17, 2011, *BBC News* online, www.bbc.com/news/uk-england-hereford-worcester-13727961.

16. *On Disgust* (Chicago: Open Court, 2004), 52–62. *On Disgust* first appeared in 1927, in a famous philosophy journal edited by the founder of phenomenology, Edmund Husserl. It defines the primary structure of the disgusting as "life out of place." This structure explains why disgust has a moral tone that is not merely exhausted by visceral aversion.

17. *An Eye for an Eye* (Cambridge: Cambridge University Press, 2007).

Chapter Eight

1. W. R. Mead, "A Crisis of Two Civilizations," *Wall Street Journal*, September 11, 2015, reproduced by the Hudson Institute as "The Roots of the Migration Crisis, www.hudson.org/research/11631-the-roots-of-the-migration-crisis.

2. See his short but interesting opuscule *The Mystery of Evil: Benedict XVI and the End of Days* (Stanford, CA: Stanford University Press, 2017).

3. *The Concept of the Political,* trans. George Schwab (Chicago: University of Chicago Press, 2007).

4. J. Huizinga. *Homo Ludens: A Study of the Play Element in Culture* (Boston: Beacon Press, 1955). Citations are to this edition.

5. See also G. McAleer, *Ecstatic Morality and Sexual Politics: A Catholic and Antitotalitarian View of the Body* (New York: Fordham University Press, 2005), 137–55. For Agamben on the archaic character of law and liturgy as games, theater, and festivals, see *The Highest Poverty,* 37, 85.

6. A. Ferguson, *An Essay on the History of Civil Society* (Cambridge: Cambridge University Press, 1996). Citations are to this edition.

7. Please see my *Tolkien and* The Lord of the Rings: *A Philosophy of War* (Amazon Digital Services, 2014).

8. Ferguson, *Essay,* 191–92.

9. Ferguson, *Essay,* 191.

10. Ferguson, *Essay,* 191.

11. Huizinga, *Homo Ludens,* 47.

12. *The Theory of Moral Sentiments* (Indianapolis: Liberty Fund, 1982), 181–82.

13. Cf. R. Sruton, *England: An Elegy* (New York: Bloomsbury, 2006), 10–11.

14. For a thoroughly Schmittean use of decision by Przywara see *AE,* 172. But see also the page immediately before, where he explores the magisterium as a requirement of the *analogia entis.*

15. A. Slowey, "Waist Management: Test-Driving Spring's Corset Trend, *Wall Street Journal,* March 2, 2017, www.wsj.com/articles/waist-management-test-driving-springs-corset-trend-1488471042.

16. R. Styles and C. McCann, "It's a Cinch! Woman Gets a Miniscule 16 Inch Waist by Sleeping in a Corset for 3 Years (and She Still Wants to Get Smaller), *Daily Mail,* June 9, 2013, www.dailymail.co.uk/femail/article-2338 647/Its-cinch-Woman-gets-miniscule-16-inch-waist-sleeping-corset-THREE -years-wants-smaller.html.

17. F. de Vitoria, *Vitoria: Political Writings,* ed. A. Pagden (Cambridge: Cambridge University Press, 2001).

18. I draw details of wealth management and tax havens from Brooke Harrington's excellent book, *Capital without Borders* (Cambridge, MA: Harvard University Press, 2016). The philosophical argument is my own.

19. I borrow the formal structure of this point from Adam Smith. See his *Theory of Moral Sentiments* (Carmel, IN: Liberty Fund, 1976), 52–53.

20. E. Burke, *Reflections on the Revolution in France* (Carmel, IN: Liberty Fund, 1999), 94.

21. Burke, *Reflections on the Revolution,* 122.

22. Burke, *Reflections on the Revolution,* 122.

Conclusion

1. J. Bentham, *Bentham: A Fragment of Government,* ed. R. Harrison (Cambridge: Cambridge University Press, 2001), 52, 55–56. See Michel Foucault's famous treatment of Bentham and the lust for "power of mind over mind," in chapter 3 of *Discipline & Punish: the Birth of the Prison* (New York: Vintage, 1979). Cf. S. Letwin, *The Pursuit of Certainty* (Carmel, IN: Liberty Fund, 1998), especially chapter 13.

2. On Kelsen, see C. Schmitt, *Political Theology* (Chicago: Chicago University Press, 2005), 18–21. In his account of Kantianism, Rawls asks that the ethically serious rely on "some anonymized version of their own life," a summation that belongs to D. Wiggins, *Ethics* (Cambridge, MA: Harvard University Press, 2006,) 282; cf. R. Scruton, *The Meaning of Conservatism* (South Bend, IN: St. Augustine's Press, 2002), 186.

3. I. Kant, *Groundwork for the Metaphysics of Morals* (New Haven, CT: Yale University Press, 2002), 43–44.

4. See *Ecstatic Morality and Sexual Politics: A Catholic and Antitotalitarian Theory of the Body* (New York: Fordham University Press, 2005); *To Kill Another: Homicide and Natural Law* (New York: Routledge, 2017); *Tolkien and* The Lord of the Rings: *A Philosophy of War* (Amazon Digital Services, 2014); and *Veneration & Refinement: The Ethics of Fashion* (2016), ethicsoffashion.com.

5. See T. Reid on the place of charades in Roman society and politics and on ritual in ancient business practice: *Thomas Reid's Lectures on the Fine Arts* (The Hague: Nijhoff, 1973), 32–33.

6. M. Merleau-Ponty, *The Primacy of Perception* (Evanston, IL: Northwestern University Press, 1982), 145–46, 117.

7. K. Wojtyla, *Love and Responsibility* (San Francisco, Ignatius, 1993).

8. A. Smith, *Theory of Moral Sentiments* (Carmel, IN: Liberty Fund, 1976), 131.

9. N. Zimmermann, *Facing the Other* (Eugene, OR: Cascade, 2015), especially chapter 3.

10. J. Prinz, *The Emotional Construction of Morals* (Oxford: Oxford University Press, 2009), 85, 167, among many others.

11. T. Malthus, *An Essay on the Principle of Population* (Cambridge: Cambridge University Press, 1992), especially 248–49.

12. For impressive evidence that beauty is a sui generis category and driver of adaptation, see R. Prum, *The Evolution of Beauty* (New York: Doubleday, 2017).

13. F. De Waal, *Primates and Philosophers* (Princeton, NJ: Princeton University Press, 2006).

14. J. Lacan, *The Triumph of Religion* (Cambridge: Polity, 2014). Cf. J. Lacan, *Seminar II* (New York: Norton, 1991), 54.

15. Kant's desire for a pure will as the linchpin to any true metaphysics of morals is also a desire for purity: "For as to what is to be morally good, it is not enough that it conform to the moral law, but it must also happen for the sake of this law" (*Groundwork*, 6). I think it is hard to deny that here Kant continues a long-standing medieval debate about whether one is moral if love for God includes any hint of self-affirmation. For my assessment of the medieval debate, please see "Pleasure: A Reflection on Benedict XVI's *Deus Caritas Est*," *Nova et Vetera: The English Edition of the International Theological Journal* 5, no. 2 (2007): 315–24.

16. K. Wojtyla, "On the Metaphysical and Phenomenological Basis of the Moral Norm," *Person and Community* (Bern: Peter Lang, 1993), 73–94.

17. T. J. Gee, "Is Fast Fashion a Class Issue? *Refinery29*, April 23, 2018, www.refinery29.uk/2017/04/149877/fast-fashion-social-issue.

18. See *The Right and the Good*, ed. P. Stratton-Lake (Oxford: Oxford University Press, 2009), 20–22.

19. See Stratton-Lake's introduction to Ross, *The Right and the Good*. See also the charge repeated in Prinz, *Emotional Construction of Morals*, 88.

20. Throughout the text, I touch on aspects of the ontology of values. Formal presentations of some of the ontology can be found in Kolnai's essays "A Defense of Intrinsicalism against 'Situation Ethics'" (*PVNS*, 265–301); and "The Concept of Hierarchy," *Ethics, Values, and Reality* (New York: Routledge, 2017), 165–85; as well as in V. Vóhanka, "The Nature and Uniqueness of Material Value-Ethics Clarified," *Ethical Perspectives* 24 (2017): 225–58.

INDEX

Graham James McAleer is professor of philosophy
at Loyola University Maryland.

CPSIA information can be obtained
at www.ICGtesting.com
Printed in the USA
LVHW081336311019
635962LV00009B/59/P

9 780268 105945